William Makepeace Thackeray

Twayne's English Authors Series

Herbert Sussman, Editor
Northeastern University

TEAS 365

WILLIAM MAKEPEACE THACKERAY
(1811–1863)
Sketch by Daniel Maclise
Reproduced by kind permission
of the Garrick Club, London

William Makepeace Thackeray

By Ina Ferris

University of Ottawa

Twayne Publishers • Boston

William Makepeace Thackeray

Ina Ferris

Copyright © 1983 by G.K. Hall & Company
All Rights Reserved
Published by Twayne Publishers
A Division of G. K. Hall & Company
70 Lincoln Street
Boston, Massachusetts 02111

Book Production by Marne B. Sultz

Book Design by Barbara Anderson

Printed on permanent/durable acid-free
paper and bound in the United States of
America.

**Library of Congress Cataloging in Publication
Data**

Ferris, Ina
William Makepeace Thackeray.

  (Twayne's English authors series; TEAS 365)
  Bibliography: p. 138
  Includes index.
  1. Thackeray, William Makepeace,
1811–1863—
Criticism and interpretation.
I. Title. II. Series.
PR5638.F47 1983 823'.8 83-184
ISBN 0-8057-6851-3

Mano Mamai ir Babai

Contents

About the Author

Ina Ferris received her Ph.D. from the University of California, Los Angeles, and is currently Assistant Professor of English at the University of Ottawa. Her publications include articles on contemporary Canadian fiction as well as on Thackeray, Walter Scott and John Fowles. She is working on a study of readers in nineteenth-century realism.

Preface

Thackeray is an obscure major novelist. Rivaling Charles Dickens at a time when the novel was central to English culture as at no period before or since, Thackeray entered the mainstream of literary history, shaping the sensibility of writers as diverse as Anthony Trollope and Walter Pater. But he has traveled less successfully into the twentieth century than his great rival whose genius continues to excite both popular and academic interest. On the basis of *Vanity Fair,* and to a lesser extent *Henry Esmond,* Thackeray is granted status as a major Victorian, but his imagination has generated neither the seriousness nor the intensity of the attention that Dickens and George Eliot have received. He remains a shadowy figure—his name familiar, his writings less so.

Thackeray's playful manner and careless air, his puzzling shifts in tone and disconcerting ironies tend to obscure the seriousness of his interest both in fiction and in the life that fiction images. This study assumes that seriousness and explores its workings in his major novels. Having to earn his living by his pen, Thackeray was a prolific writer, pouring out assorted satiric sketches, stories, essays, lectures, travel books, ballads, and Christmas books in addition to the six long novels. I have preferred to interpret Thackeray's career by concentrating on the early works most significant for his development and on the six novels, devoting more space than customary to *The Newcomes* and *The Adventures of Philip,* two works but recently emerging from the shade cast by *Vanity Fair* and *Henry Esmond.* Much that is sparkling and intriguing had necessarily to be omitted, but restriction has allowed a sharper focus on the central problem in Thackeray: his self-conscious realism.

For his contemporaries Thackeray's name was synonymous with a realist fidelity to experience, and his entire career was powered by the realist question: how can fiction respond to and reflect contemporary reality? The question is complex and so was Thackeray's understanding. He established Victorian realism in *Vanity Fair,* but his skeptical mind continued to probe the problem: to question the nature of reality and the nature of narrative. It led him, particularly in his later work, to sophisticated and subtle—if sometimes despairing—investigations of the assumptions and limits of the realist mode. His investigations, it must be stressed, were not theoretical or intellectual but intuitive, motivated by his abiding concern that fiction be committed to the complications of human living.

For so avid a reader of novels and so self-conscious a writer as Thackeray, the appropriate context for understanding his own thinking about his art is the formal context of the novel as a genre. Accordingly, after a brief outline of contemporary critical reaction to the novel in question (including Thackeray's own), each chapter typically identifies the informing fictional tradition for that particular work, as with the *Bildungsroman* for *Pendennis* or the quixotic novel for *The Newcomes*. The range of traditions on which Thackeray draws conveys his awareness of the rich possibilities of the novel and his sense of it as a form. More than most Victorians he recognized the conventional basis of literature, struggling against convention in the name of realism but knowing all the while that he was only creating new conventions.

Many readers have written wisely about Thackeray and to them all I owe a debt not always acknowledged sufficiently in the footnotes. For their personal encouragement of my work on Thackeray, I am warmly grateful to Alexander Welsh, who challenged my thinking, and to Juliet McMaster, who gracefully expanded it. Herbert Sussman, my editor, and Diane Lebrun, who typed the manuscript, both eased my way through the book and I thank them. Most of all I thank my husband, Stephen, who listened with patience and responded with intelligence but still reads Dickens.

Ina Ferris

University of Ottawa

Acknowledgments

I wish to thank Harvard University Press for permission to quote from *The Letters and Private Papers of William Makepeace Thackeray,* edited by Gordon N. Ray, copyright 1945 by Hester Thackeray Ritchie Fuller and the President and Fellows of Harvard College.

Chronology

1846–1847   *The Snobs of England (Punch)*, retitled *The Book of Snobs* in book form (1848).

1847   *Punch's Prize Novelists* (retitled *Novels by Eminent Hands* in book form, 1856).

1847–1848   *Vanity Fair* (January 1847–July 1848).

1848   Friendship with Jane Brookfield, wife of the Reverend William Brookfield, deepens.

1848–1850   *The History of Pendennis* (November 1848–December 1850).

1850   *Rebecca and Rowena.*

1851   Lectures on humorists of eighteenth century in London (published as *The English Humourists of the Eighteenth Century* in 1853). Break with Jane Brookfield.

1852   *The History of Henry Esmond.*

1852–1853   First American tour.

1855   *The Rose and the Ring.*

1855–1856   Second American tour, lectures on the Hanoverian kings (published as *The Four Georges* in 1860).

1857   Runs unsuccessfully for the Oxford seat in Parliament.

1857–1859   *The Virginians* (November 1857–October 1859).

1859–1862   Editor of *Cornhill Magazine.*

1860   *Lovel the Widower* in *Cornhill.*

1860–1863   *Roundabout Papers* in *Cornhill.*

1863   Begins *Denis Duval* (unfinished, published posthumously in *Cornhill* in 1864).

1863   Dies December 24 in London.

Chapter One
A Man of the World

"Our books are diaries," Thackeray wrote near the end of his life, "in which our own feelings must of necessity be set down."[1] More than most Victorian novelists, he stressed the interrelationship of his life and his fiction, telling his mother, for example, that his hero, Henry Esmond, was "a handsome likeness of an ugly son of yours",[2] signing letters throughout his life with the names of various of his characters like Michael Angelo Titmarsh or Arthur Pendennis, and inserting caricatures of himself into illustrations of his novels. Such self-identification can obscure as much as reveal, of course, and William Makepeace Thackeray remains an elusive figure, shrouding himself in the irony of which he was so gifted a practitioner. We do well to remember his lifelong fondness for puns—those jokes that depend on the existence of at least a double meaning. But it is at least clear that some knowledge of his life is an essential preliminary to a study of his work. And underlying the variety of incidents, roles, and attitudes that characterized his existence, one mark persists: in different ways Thackeray was all his life an outsider who looked very much like an insider. The peculiar tensions of such a position created the distinctive Thackerayan voice which amused, enraged, and enlightened the Victorian public.

Thackeray belongs to the mid-Victorian generation whose achievements represent the high point of Victorian culture. He was born in 1811, his rival Charles Dickens in 1812. Charles Darwin and Alfred Tennyson were both born in 1809, while Robert Browning was the same age as Dickens. In the same year that Thackeray published his first great novel, *Vanity Fair* (1847), Emily Bronte published *Wuthering Heights,* her sister, Charlotte, *Jane Eyre,* and Dickens made important new strides in his fiction with *Dombey and Son.* An enormously gifted generation, it was also a troubled one, and William Makepeace Thackeray is one of its most representative members.

The Early Years

Thackeray was born into an upper-middle-class family that numbered various important professionals among its members but whose most significant alliance was a long and profitable Indian connection.[3] The grandfather, after whom Thackeray was named, had made a sizeable fortune as Collector of Sylhet with the East India Company, but the Thackerays tended to have large families and the novelist's father, Richmond Thackeray—one of eleven children—had to make his own way. After being educated at Eton, Richmond sailed out to India where he rose rapidly in the East India Company and lived (to English eyes) in exotic splendor in Calcutta, employing upwards of sixty servants. At the age of twenty-eight on October 13, 1810, he married eighteen-year-old Anne Becher whose roots were also Anglo-Indian and who had been sent to Calcutta to recover from a love affair in England. At fifteen Anne had fallen in love with a young soldier, but her grandmother had disapproved of the young man's prospects. After several attempts to break off the relationship (including locking Anne in her room), the grandmother informed the girl that her lover was dead. Anne met and married Richmond Thackeray shortly afterwards and before she was nineteen gave birth to her only child, William, born in Calcutta on July 18, 1811.

His birth made Thackeray a member of the increasingly dominant middle class in English culture, yet it also set him apart from boys of his own class in England by providing him with a perpspective unavailable to most of them. Not only did he spend his first five years in India but when he came to England, he mingled with Anglo-Indians who formed a world of their own and saw mainstream English society from a particular, more distanced angle. Thus the pattern of being both inside and outside appears early in Thackeray's life. He retained little memory of his early years in Calcutta but his fiction is filled with Anglo-Indian characters, ranging from the pompous, obese Jos Sedley in *Vanity Fair* to the engaging Colonel Newcome in *The Newcomes*. As an only child Thackeray was pampered, but his life was not all ease, for he was initiated early into the experience of loss. His father died in 1815 when Thackeray was four, and he lost his mother in a fashion as well. The time had come for him to be sent to England—the Indian climate was supposed to be bad for English children—and his mother could not go with him. The young soldier whom Anne had loved and thought dead, Henry Carmichael-Smyth, turned out to be very much alive and living in India. When her husband died, she promised to marry Henry after the eighteen-month period of mourning. In the meantime young Thackeray's departure could not be delayed, so in December 1816 Anne reluctantly placed her five-and-a-half-year-old son on a ship for England. The trauma of the separation remained with Thackeray, who recorded similar partings in his novels and who avoided partings himself as an adult whenever possible.

Severed abruptly from his home and mother, the young boy set off on a voyage of almost five months which was enlivened by a glimpse of the exiled Napoleon on St. Helena. After arrival in England, he settled into a period of misery and loneliness. He was sent to a dreadful school in Southampton where he was so unhappy that, he later recorded, "I remember kneeling by my little bed of a night, and saying, 'Pray God, I may dream of my mother!'" ("On Letts's Diary," *Roundabout Papers*). He was soon transferred to a rather more congenial school run by his mother's cousin, the Reverend John Turner, in Chiswick where he stayed for the next three years. But the loneliness remained. What those years meant to Thackeray may be inferred from his moving portrayal of the solitary and insecure young Henry Esmond in *The History of Henry Esmond*. Suggestively, the young hero has lost his mother and responds with passionate devotion to the appearance of a radiant mother-figure in the first scene of the novel. Thackeray himself did not see his mother for three and a half years. When she and her husband returned to England in July 1820, she described her son's reaction to her own mother: "dear soul he has a perfect recollection of me he could not speak but kissed me & looked at me again & again."[4] Henceforth, as Thackeray's biographer, Gordon Ray, points out, Thackeray saw life as "a dichotomy between the warmth and trust of a happy home circle and the brutality or indifference of the outside world."[5] This early experience accounts for his own consistent sensitivity to children and, more important, for the particular ideal of woman and the prominence of domestic values that we find in his novels.

Thackeray's mother dominated his emotional life until late adolescence and continued to be an important force until his death. Anne Carmichael-Smyth was a strong, attractive woman who loved her only son with an intense, possessive love which was to be both an anchor and a burden to Thackeray for the rest of his life. He captured her power and his own ambivalence in the portrait of Helen Pendennis in *Pendennis,* one of the most incisive anatomies of maternal love in English fiction. Like Helen Pendennis, his mother was intensely jealous of anyone (particularly any woman) who threatened her position with her son; not surprisingly, Thackeray's relations with her after adolescence were marked increasingly by struggle. "When I was a boy at Larkbeare," he commented in 1852, "I thought her an Angel & worshipped her. I see but a woman now, O so tender so loving so cruel" (*Letters,* 3:13). Thackeray's insight into the complexities of family love owes a good deal to his experience with his mother, as do his sharp analyses of righteous virtue in novels like *Vanity Fair* and *The Newcomes.*

The most frequent subject of his battles with his mother was her religion. She adhered to a fierce and rigid Evangelicalism whose doctrines and absolutism Thackeray distrusted, at least partly because he saw in them a life-destroying potential. "How you would have gone off singing to be roasted!" he told his mother dryly in 1853, adding: "You are made of the materials of w[hich] Martyrs and persecutors are made—You persecute with tears and maternal pangs" (*Letters,* 3:217). To his elder daughter, Anne, he explained that once "dogmatic belief" is admitted, "pain, cruelty, persecution, separation of dear relatives, follow as a matter of course" (*Letters,* 3:94). He regarded as "awful presumption" his mother's conviction that she had "the true Faith" and pointed out repeatedly the arrogance of this stand (*Letters,* 2:205). Thackeray himself valued Christ and the New Testament but read the Bible as "a book" and not "an Oracle" *Letters,* 3:218), and he disliked intensely the Old Testament which "contains no Gentleness no Humility no forgiveness—nothing but exclusiveness and pride curses and arrogance" (*Letters,* 2:206). Thackeray's adult skepticism, tolerance, and frank enjoyment of the vanities of the world (like claret and cigars) can therefore be seen as largely reactions to the excesses of a mother whom he still continued to love profoundly.

The Schooling of a Gentleman

While Thackeray's relationship with his mother was dominating his inner life, he was simultaneously developing the outward manner of an English gentleman and learning to cope with the world of his peers. The process began when he was ten years old. On January 15, 1822, he entered Charterhouse, the prestigious London public school which his stepfather had attended and which Thackeray was to fictionalize in numerous writings, bitterly as Slaughter House in *Men's Wives* and more genially as Greyfriars in *Pendennis* and *The Newcomes.* At the time, Charterhouse was badly run, heavily reliant on discipline by flogging (Thackeray's fictional teachers have names like Dr. Birch and Mr. Swishtail), and its notorious headmaster, Dr. John Russell, identified teaching with humiliation and force. Thackeray was made to feel inferior and his first years at the school were miserable, although later he became tolerably content in a circle of friends who had a lively interest in the literature of the day. The Charterhouse experience marked Thackeray in several ways, not the least of which was its impact on his face. In a fight staged apparently to amuse some bored senior boys on a rainy day, Thackeray had his nose broken by George Venables who—in proper public school tradition—became a lifelong friend. In response to the brutalities of public school, Thackeray developed defenses to protect his sensitive inner nature and to give him a sense of ease in the world.[6] He adopted the role of a lazy, good-tempered boy who liked to eat and had a talent for caricature. In the rough and tumble boys' world the future satirist was born as he amused fellow students by drawing caricatures of teachers and writing parodies of popular sentimental verses.

After six and a half years at Charterhouse, Thackeray continued the education of a gentleman by entering Trinity College, Cambridge, in February 1829 where he lived in the same building that had housed Sir Isaac Newton and the popular historian, Thomas Babington Macaulay. Alfred Tennyson, a few years older, was a fellow student. But Thackeray was not destined to make a name for himself at Trinity College. Like his autobiographical hero, Arthur Pendennis, he was exhilarated by the freedom of university life and spent most of his time drinking at wine parties, lounging, or taking lazy walks. He attended few lectures, though he vowed constantly to reform and apply himself to serious study—tomorrow. For most of his life, in fact, Thackeray was to be continually repenting and resolving to be more disciplined, to eat less, and so on. His first trip to Paris in the summer of 1829 did little to make him a more conscientious student. There he plunged into the delights of theater and—more ominously—those of the gambling table. At the famous salon of Frascati's he found rouge et noir "so powerful that I could not tear myself away until I lost my last piece—I dreamed of it all night" (*Letters,* 1:90–91). Although he reassured his mother that he would not go again, the reassurance proved to be hollow.

When Thackeray returned to Cambridge in the fall, he gave full vent to the epicurean side of his nature and moved with a fast crowd, drinking and gambling. On one occasion he was fleeced by professional gamblers, losing £1,500 which he promised to pay when he received the inheritance that his father had left in trust for him. He sneaked off for pleasure trips to London and even to Paris. Thackeray did engage in more respectable pastimes as well, contributing to a college journal, *The Gownsman,* and joining a debating society. One of his closest friends was an intense young clergyman, John Allen, a choice which suggests that Thackeray's more serious side had not gone underground completely. But his academic activities were minimal and by the end of Easter term, 1830, he had decided that "deep meditations on angles & parallelograms" were a waste of time and he left the university.

His Parisian adventures had instilled a desire to travel, so in July 1830 he set off for Germany, ending up in Weimar (the Pumpernickel of *Vanity Fair*) where he met the aged Goethe and spent six months reading German literature, attending balls at court, and engaging in playful flirtations. On his return to England in the spring of 1831 he decided to try the law and entered the Middle Temple of the Inns of Court. As at Cambridge, he soon lost any ambition and drifted into a lazy, bohemian life of idleness, theater-going, drinking, and gambling. "The day spent in seediness repentance & novel reading," Thackeray begins a typical diary entry from this period. After listing the novels, he concludes: "I did nothing else all day except eat biscuits, a very excellent amusement & not so expensive as some other—" (*Letters*, 1:206). On July 18, 1832, Thackeray turned twenty-one and came into the money his father had left him, around £20,000, a portion of which went to pay his considerable gambling debts. He celebrated his majority with a trip to Paris and for the next sixteen months spent money freely. All this ended when toward the end of 1833 his fortune was lost in the collapse of the Indian agency-houses and the young gentleman of property suddenly lost his position.

Marriage and Journalism

The disappearance of his inheritance, however, seems to have relieved Thackeray. It rescued him from a life of dissipation which had been filling him with self-dissatisfaction. So Philip Firmin is energized by a similar loss in *The Adventures of Philip*. Thackeray now turned to working on a long-held ambition to be a painter, studying first in London, then in Paris where he stayed with his formidable grandmother, Mrs. Butler, who had led an unconventional life in India and Europe and who became the model for Miss Crawley in *Vanity Fair*. As an art student, Thackeray continued the bohemian existence he had developed as a law student but now enjoyed the life thoroughly. To be a young artist in Paris, he later wrote, is to enjoy "the easiest, merriest, dirtiest existence possible" ("On The French School of Painting," *The Paris Sketch Book*). But by early 1835 Thackeray had to recognize that he lacked the talent to be an artist. He fell into a depression from which he was rescued this time by love.

In the summer of 1835 he met eighteen-year-old Isabella Shawe who, like Thackeray, had been born in India (where her father had served as a colonel) but whose family roots were Irish rather than English. Isabella was living in Paris with her mother, a widow with five children who resented the narrow means and loss of status resulting from her husband's death. A high-strung, possessive woman, Mrs. Shawe dominated the timid, childlike Isabella and discouraged her daughter's involvement with the impecunious Thackeray. Her tactics may be inferred from Thackeray's explosion in a letter to Isabella: "but what in God's name have I been saying to hurt you . . . and your Mother?—What a scoundrel should I be were I to endeavour to weaken such a tie as exists between you two—The separation to w[hich] I alluded did not go farther than the bedroom—If I recollect rightly this was the chief object of my thoughts at the moment" (*Letters*, 1:309). Such candid talk of bedrooms seems to have terrified Isabella, but she overcame her fears sufficiently to consider herself engaged to Thackeray in the spring of 1836. Mrs. Shawe continued her efforts and by July wore down her daughter who broke the engagement. Thackeray smuggled in a letter whereupon (in a sequence re-created in *The Adventures of Philip*) Isabella roused herself to defy her mother and then collapsed. Mrs. Shawe capitulated and attended the wedding of the couple at the British embassy in Paris on August 20, 1836.

Shortly after his marriage, Thackeray moved to London where he could earn a living at journalism. So began a ten-year period (1837–47) when he worked as a freelancer in the rough, low-status world of journalism. "Magazine work is below street sweeping as a trade," complained Thomas Carlyle in 1831.[7] Thackeray, educated as a gentleman, was doubly alienated: from his fellow journalists whose social origins were not usually gentlemanly, and from the class to which he felt he still belonged but from which his profession barred him. Such alienation allowed him to see the social order with particular sharpness, as both his journalism and novels attest. Thackeray's life during this decade was a frantic one as he rushed to meet deadlines and to find new assignments. He wrote on books, pictures, and social mores, produced satires, burlesques, and assorted types of fiction. From 1837 to 1844 he worked mostly for *Fraser's Magazine* where he created memorable characters like Charles James Yellowplush, Esq., who discoursed comically on such things as "Fashnable Fax and Polite Annygoats." On the whole Thackeray was exhilarated by the energy and pressure of his way of life. London, he wrote in 1839, is "rare fun for a man with broad shoulders who can push through the crowd" (*Letters*, 1:397).

He needed those broad shoulders in 1840 when his wife became insane and his home life collapsed. The Thackeray marriage seems to have been a happy one but there were difficulties. Isabella, in particular, lived under a good deal of strain. She was weakened by three quick pregnancies: Anne was born in June 1837, Jane in July 1838, Harriet Marian (Minny) in May 1840. The second daughter, Jane, lived only eight months, and her death in March 1839 left both parents grieving deeply. To heighten these pressures, the two formidable mothers-in-law hated each other, while Thackeray and Mrs. Shawe were barely civil, so creating a conflict of loyalties in Isabella. Worst of all, she began to feel herself an unworthy wife, especially when her husband started to spend more and more time away from home. Thackeray took to working in clubs—an enduring habit—in order to escape the constant interruptions of his wife and Anny, but Isabella no doubt sensed that part of his motive in fleeing was the desire for more intellectual and worldly companionship than she could provide.

After the birth of her third daughter, Isabella fell into a deep depression and in August 1840 things came to a crisis. Thackeray decided to go to Belgium to write some articles, hoping to capitalize on the modest success of his recently published first book, *The Paris Sketch Book* (1840). Isabella begged him not to go, but Thackeray failed to perceive the gravity of her state and departed cheerfully. "My head flies away with me as if it were a balloon," Isabella wrote at this time (*Letters,* 1:462). When Thackeray returned, he was alarmed at her condition and took her first to the seaside and then to Ireland in the hope that her mother and sister might be able to help restore her health while he worked on an Irish book under contract to Chapman and Hall.

On the trip to Ireland, Isabella tried to drown herself, and for the first time Thackeray recognized the extent of her illness. Once in Ireland his bitterness against Mrs. Shawe was inflamed when she did not give the kind of help he had expected, suggested that Isabella be put in a madhouse, and insulted Thackeray himself. Such experiences with Mrs. Shawe are responsible for what Lambert Ennis calls "the terrible row of mothers-in-law that stalks through [Thackeray's] books like the dumb show in *Macbeth.*"[8] In this crisis his own mother came through splendidly, taking in his family while Isabella was receiving treatment. For over a year Thackeray continued to hope for her recovery, trying different forms of therapy, but in February 1842 he admitted defeat. After a period at a French asylum, Isabella was transferred to private care in England where, Thackeray noted in 1848, "that poor little wife of mine . . . does not care [twopence] for anything but her dinner and her glass of porter" (*Letters*, 2:440). This painful experience found its way into his novels, particularly in the depiction of Amelia's near-madness on the eve of Waterloo in *Vanity Fair*. Isabella herself outlived her husband by more than thirty years, dying in 1894.

From the age of twenty-nine Thackeray was a quasi-widower: a family man without a wife yet unable to replace the loss. Isabella's illness left an enduring void. "A man without a woman," Thackeray wrote eighteen years later, "is a lonely wretch" (*Letters*, 4:81). Even though he soon renewed his gregarious existence, dining out and resuming the life of a bon vivant, he was once again between worlds—neither bachelor nor husband. From this period stems his habit of presenting himself as someone much older, doomed to be an observer rather than participant in life, a stance which characterizes his narrators as well. Furthermore, the loss of Isabella deepened the melancholy that his early childhood had induced, darkening the urbane, worldly tone that marked his public voice and giving his narrators their distinctive modulation.

Vanity Fair and Success

From 1842 to 1846 Thackeray lived alone in London, while his daughters stayed with his mother in Paris. Increasingly, his most important writing was done for *Punch* where he had his first real success, a satiric series, "The Snobs of England, by One of Themselves" (1846–47). While "Snobs" was running, he finally succeeded in setting up a home for his daughters in Kensington. They came to live with him in the fall of 1846, a reunion which left Thackeray an appreciably happier man.[9] He took up a story that he had begun in 1845, "The Novel Without a Hero: Pen and Pencil Sketches of English Society," and transformed it into *Vanity Fair* which appeared in yellow-covered monthly parts from January 1847 to June 1848. With the publication of *Vanity Fair* Thackeray's days as a minor journalist were over. "I am become a sort of great man in my way," he told his mother in January 1848, explaining that he was now "at the top of the tree . . . and having a great fight up there with Dickens" (*Letters*, 2:333). Indeed from now on Thackeray and Dickens were recognized as the preeminent novelists of their time, and Thackeray became a literary lion whose manners made him acceptable even in aristocratic circles.

He enjoyed it all immensely, but as he set to work on his second major novel, *Pendennis* (1848–50), he was absorbed in a private rather than public world. From 1848 to 1851 his inner world was dominated by Jane

Brookfield, the wife of an old Cambridge friend, William Brookfield, now a clergyman. When Jane married the thirty-two-year-old William at the age of twenty in 1841,'he treated her rather like a favorite pupil and she worshiped him. But as career disappointments mounted and their childlessness continued, William began to neglect Jane and to treat her with coldness. Thackeray had met Jane in 1842 but remained primarily William's friend until October 1848 when Jane confessed to him her loneliness and unhappiness. Thackeray reciprocated with the revelation of his own bleak state, and—typically Victorian—they vowed to be "brother" and "sister" to one another, though Thackeray's feelings were more than fraternal.

Until 1851 he visited Jane constantly and poured out his heart and mind in long letters, finding in her a much-needed outlet for repressed emotions and a way to fill partially the emptiness left by Isabella. Jane's own feelings are less clear, but her primary allegiance was always to her husband. When he demanded that she cut off all connection with Thackeray in the summer of 1851, Jane obeyed, leaving Thackeray feeling bitter and betrayed: "I have been played with by a woman, and flung over at a beck from the lord and master" (*Letters*, 4:431). The rupture remained "a tremendous amputation" and widened the split between external and internal in Thackeray: "though I go about and grin from party to party & dinner to dinner . . . I have a natural hang dog melancholy within" (*Letters*, 3:813). In September 1851 at the height of the Brookfield crisis he began writing *The History of Henry Esmond* (1852) which resonates with the love and loss of Jane and which Thackeray dourly described as "a book of cutthroat melancholy suitable to my state" (*Letters*, 2:807).

Restless after finishing the novel, he left for a lecture tour of the United States in October 1852. He stayed there six months, speaking on the eighteenth-century English humorists, a series which he had already delivered successfully in England in 1851. The visit proved a beneficial diversion from the Brookfield affair. Thackeray's lectures were well received and he was delighted with Americans, most notably with nineteen-year-old Sally Baxter, a lively New York beauty with whom he flirted playfully and who lies behind Ethel Newcome, the vivacious heroine of his next novel, *The Newcomes* (1853–55). "It's not good. It's stupid," Thackeray complained in writing this book (Letters, 3:299), as he complained in writing most of his novels, but *The Newcomes* proved to be the summit of his achievement. He began the novel shortly after his return from the United States while on a European tour with his daughters. When in Rome on this trip he suffered his first bout of malaria, and this marks the beginning of the ill health that was to plague him in the last decade of his life.

In this decade Thackeray's daughters, Anny and Minny, became the emotional center of his life. He was a sensitive, generous parent whom both girls loved deeply; they, in turn, sustained and motivated their father. His concern for their financial security after his death, in fact, became an obsession and Thackeray labored furiously to replace for them the inheritance he had lost as a young man. Finding lecturing profitable, he launched a second American tour in 1855, this time speaking on English royalty in a series later published as *The Four Georges* (1860). In 1856–57 he took "these astonishing Georges" on an extended tour of England and Scotland, persisting in lecturing in spite of poor health because, as he told his mother, "it rains money" (*Letters,* 4:8).

It rained more money in April 1859 when Thackeray accepted the offer of the publisher, George Smith, to become editor of a new magazine, *Cornhill Magazine,* a position he held until his resignation in March 1862 when what he called the "thorns in the cushion" became too prickly. He also wrote for the journal, providing fiction (*Lovel the Widower,* 1860; *The Adventures of Philip,* 1861–62) and a series of familiar essays, *Roundabout Papers* (1860–63). Through the *Cornhill* Thackeray gave an important impetus to the career of Anthony Trollope, and the magazine featured such illustrious names as Alfred Tennyson, John Ruskin, and Matthew Arnold. The *Cornhill* was an enormous success, its first number (January 1860) selling a record 120,000 copies. In gratitude George Smith doubled his editor's already generous stipend. Thackeray had succeeded in his efforts; he had replaced the patrimony lost in 1833.

Toward the end of his life Thackeray became increasingly tired of writing fiction, declaring that "the novel-writing vein is used up" and that he had "nothing fresh to say" (*Letters,* 4:271, 242n). He planned to write a history of the period of Queen Anne, but in the event the closest he came to it was in building a magnificent Queen Anne house at 2 Palace Green, Kensington, where he lived from March 1862 until his death. In his final year he continued to frequent his clubs and to eat good dinners but was often tired and ill. On December 23, 1863, he was confined to bed and died that night in the early hours of Christmas Eve, leaving behind his grief-stricken mother and daughters. He was fifty-two years old. Two years earlier Thackeray had written: "The terminus can't be far off—a few years more or less. I wouldn't care to travel over the ground again: though I have had some pleasant days and dear companions" (*Letters,* 4:247).

Chapter Two
The Making of the Novelist

In his decade (1837–47) as a freelance writer Thackeray produced dozens of stories, sketches, reviews, and essays, supplemented by drawings and light verse. Their subjects range from capital punishment to the celebrated fish stew, *bouillabaisse,* from camels in Smyrna to sordid English marriages. Through having to cope with such a variety of themes and forms Thackeray developed the stylistic dexterity that was to distinguish him as a novelist.

He experimented with different narrators, mimicking now a prententious footman (Charles James Yellowplush), now an indolent gourmand (Fat Contributor), now a self-deprecating painter (Michael Angelo Titmarsh). The voice of Titmarsh in particular allowed Thackeray great flexibility of tone, and Titmarsh became his favorite early narrator. He narrates Thackeray's best travel book, *Notes of a Journey From Cornhill to Grand Cairo* (1846), a volume noteworthy for its diversity of tone within an overall consistency of outlook. *Cornhill to Cairo* is shot through with the deflating humor characteristic of Thackeray (the famed Pyramids are dismissed as "two big ones and a little one," ch. 15), but it also includes humor of a more whimsical variety, meditations both serious and playful, and harsh reportorial realism. Controlling the shifting rhythms and tones is a constant purpose: to counteract romantic literary images of the East. Musing about the Crusades, Titmarsh asks: "When shall we have a real account of those times and heroes—no good-humoured pageant, like those of the [Walter] Scott romances? (ch. 8).

This question is central to all of Thackeray's art. To provide "a real account" not only of the past but of the present is his primary motive as a writer. From the beginning his work attempts to correct what he considers to be the false view of reality implied in the popular novels of his day. His early writing is especially aggressive in this respect, and the world that he presents in reaction to the sentimental, idealized world of popular novels is thoroughly brutal and sordid. As a result, the early Thackeray was usually charged with a distorting bitterness: "too severe and biting" commented the *Spectator* in 1840, and eight years later the generally admiring George Henry Lewes continued the criticism by asserting that Thackeray's skepticism was "pushed too far."[1] But what "pushed" Thackeray was less skepticism about life than skepticism about literature. Like so many novelists, Thackeray began his career by writing novels against other novels. In other words—like Henry Fielding and Jane Austen—he began as a parodist. And the key to parody, as James H. Wheatley reminds us, is the recognition "that there is a profound connection between the language a man uses and his way of thinking about himself and the world."[2]

The Newgate Novel and *Catherine*

Thackeray and Bulwer-Lytton. The type of fiction that particularly incensed the young Thackeray and led to his own first extended fiction, *Catherine* (1839–40), was the Newgate novel. These novels flourished in the 1830s and typically focused on the life of a criminal who was (or could be) found in *The Newgate Calendar,* a well-known collection of criminal biographies. Edward Bulwer-Lytton set the trend with *Paul Clifford* in 1830 and soon novels about thieves, highwaymen, and murderers were pouring out of the presses and being dramatized on stage.[3] Thackeray was one of the earliest, most persistent, and effective critics of this school of fiction which tended to distort historical facts and to idealize and glamorize criminal life. Thackeray was outraged not only because of the moral implications but because to him novels were in a sense histories. Perhaps, he mused, they were in effect "truer than real histories," for a novel like Fielding's *Tom Jones* gave "a better idea of the state and ways of the people" than "authentic histories" of the period ("On Some French Fashionable Novels," *Paris Sketch Book*). Newgate novels, however, were fakes. They pretended to portray "low life" but created only "the sham low" which catered to the middle-class reader, putting comfortable old ideas into the titillating, exotic mouths of prostitutes and murderers.[4]

In his campaign against the Newgate novel, Thackeray's main specific target was Edward Bulwer-Lytton and his novel, *Eugene Aram* (1832). Aram was a schoolmaster, reputedly gentle and highly intelligent, who was executed in 1759 for killing a man for money. In the novel Bulwer elevates Aram's social status, omits the wife and seven children deserted by the actual Aram, and turns him into a High Tragic Hero who rids the earth of a "low and creeping thing" and sees murder as "a great and solemn sacrifice to Knowledge."[5] These are, admittedly, the more vulnerable parts of Bulwer's novel, but his elevation and mystification of the hero and his act shape the entire work. Not surprisingly, Thackeray responded to *Eugene Aram* in 1832 by calling it "humbug" and "eloquent clap-trap" (*Letters,* 1:198).

This opinion did not change. When Thackeray became a writer himself, Bulwer was a favorite target in his reviews and sketches. Bulwer's notorious manner ("In the divine Priesthood of the Beautiful . . .")[6] made him especially susceptible to Thackeray's "slashing" pen, and he is the object of Thackeray's most famous parody, "George de Barnwell," published in *Punch* in 1847 (reprinted in *Novels by Eminent Hands*). For his parody Thackeray takes the well-known English story of George Barnwell, the apprentice who robbed his employer and murdered his uncle, and turns him into George de Barnwell, whose pursuit of "the Lofty and the Ideal" enables him to brush aside the reality of his actions. From the devastating opening ("In the Morning of Life the Truthful wooed the Beautiful . . .") to the hero's final dismissal of his victim as "a sordid worm," Thackeray punctures Bulwer with skill, exposing the vanity, arrogance, and emptiness of his fictional world.

Although part of Thackeray's response to Bulwer stems from a characteristic distrust of any attitude of moral superiority, part reflects a more general quarrel between two important and opposing theories of art. Thackeray stands on the side of realism: art is the imitation of everyday experience. Bulwer, on the other hand, upholds idealism: art imagines what could be. The difference may be measured by their contrasting attitudes to the relationship between nature (the external world) and art. Thackeray seems to have formulated his ideas first in connection with painting, and his art reviews are especially helpful in clarifying his realist approach.[7] In them Thackeray calls repeatedly for an end to the "heroic" style of art and to "the classical humbug" that sustains it. In its place he proposes actual observation of nature as the source of models and standards (e.g., "On the French School of Painting," *Paris Sketch Book*). To Bulwer in contrast "the Natural" is merely "the Commonplace," and in art "Nature is not to be copied but exalted."[8] In the nineteenth century it was Thackeray's view that came to dominate the novel not only in England but on the Continent as well.

Catherine (1839–40).   The quarrel with Bulwer and with Newgate fiction produced Thackeray's first long work, *Catherine,* which is both a serious parody of and alternative to the criminal romance. An intentionally harsh and mean book, *Catherine* is Thackeray's "real account" of a criminal life. The story is narrated by Ikey Solomons who presents his narrative as a "cathartic" which he hopes will induce a "wholesome nausea" in readers "poisoned by the prevailing style of literary practice" ("Another Last Chapter"). For this "cathartic" Thackeray turned to the story of Catherine Hayes in *The Newgate Calendar*. Hayes was executed in 1726 for participating in the murder of her husband with two accomplices, one of whom was supposedly her illegitimate son and—it was rumored—lover. The murder was a grisly job, involving chopping off the head (which Catherine Hayes originally recommended boiling to prevent recognition) and dismembering the rest of the body.[9] This was a far cry from the genteel Eugene Aram or the dashing Jack Sheppard, and in *Catherine* Thackeray uses the brutal details to hammer home his point.[10] Even so, he felt in the end that "it was not made disgusting enough" (*Letters*, 1:433).

Catherine opens with the declaration that what follows will obey fashion in being "agreeably low, delightfully disgusting," and the story itself observes the conventions of the Newgate novel but strips them of their sentiment and glamor. At a country inn Catherine Hall, an illiterate, vain, and attractive servant exploited by the landlady, meets a vain and stupid army officer, Count von Galgenstein. She becomes his mistress and bears him a son, but the count tires of her and schemes to marry a wealthy woman. Catherine learns of his plan from Corporal Brock, a selfish and clever scoundrel whom the count also plans to discard. Catherine tries to poison the count, Brock takes advantage of the count's sickness to steal his money, and Catherine flees. Ending up in her home village, she marries John Hayes, a spindly, miserly carpenter who has long loved her. Shortly after the marriage, Hayes is kidnapped by a gang headed by Brock (now calling himself Wood) and is ransomed by a typically doting Thackerayan mother.

After several years Catherine and Hayes move to London where Hayes becomes a moneylender. He and Catherine quarrel frequently, and Catherine's loutish son, Tom, does little to improve domestic harmony. Wood (the former Brock) becomes their lodger and fuels family tensions for amusement. When Count von Galgenstein reappears, Catherine convinces herself that only her repellent husband stands in the way of marriage to the count. Hayes is killed by Wood and Tom, with Catherine looking on. The next night she meets the count, but her marital hopes are dashed when he sees Hayes's head on a post and collapses into permanent insanity. In the original version Thackeray included newspaper accounts of the murder and of the subsequent death of Catherine, but these are omitted in the version usually reprinted. *Catherine* closes with a moral defense of the work where the light sarcasm of the opening ("delightfully disgusting") gives way to direct and serious statement. The narrator declares that in his book vice and virtue cannot be confused since he has presented "a scene of unmixed rascality."

This assertion that *Catherine* gives us "unmixed rascality" has long caused controversy, and Thackeray himself admitted to developing "a sneaking kindness" for his heroine (*Letters,* 1:433). Why he did so remains unclear, for Catherine is consistently unappealing. But Thackeray does relieve the brutality of the story with touches of wit and humor, and he introduces a more appealing rogue in Ensign Macshane, who serves under Brock-Wood. Catherine herself is capable of a strong feeling for her son, and John Hayes's love for her is genuine. But Thackeray's point in all this has often been misunderstood. He is not relieving the rascality of his characters so much as he is trying to give a fuller sense of their reality. One of his complaints about Newgate fiction was that it failed to give the complete truth about its heroes, brushing over their violence and meanness. To make them entirely brutal in reaction would merely propagate another "sham." In defining John Hayes's love for Catherine, for example, Thackeray tells his reader: "No mistake can be greater than that of fancying such great emotions of love are only felt by virtuous or exalted men" (ch. 1).

But love does not redeem Hayes (as it does in sentimental novels), and Thackeray makes clear that he remains basically selfish and mean. So it is with all the central characters whose fundamental viciousness is always in sight. Although Thackeray has some difficulties with irony and his handling of the narrator is uncertain, the book as a whole delivers a firm moral judgment, containing none of the ambiguities found in a novel like *Eugene Aram.* Thackeray consistently undermines the mystique of crime, insisting on its physical reality and its banality. He underlines, for example, that Catherine's search for poison leads her not to a mysterious sorceress but to an ordinary druggist. And the same chapter offers a digression that sums up his desire to "act honestly" by painting "such thieves as they are: not dandy, poetical, rose-water thieves" who "quote Plato like Eugene Aram" or "die whitewashed saints" like Nancy in Dickens's *Oliver Twist* (ch. 3).

Thackeray's target in *Catherine* extends beyond the Newgate novels themselves to include their readers. In this inclusion of the reader in the moral analysis of the fiction Thackeray establishes a pattern which he will make a trademark of all his novels. Where Newgate fiction typically turned the criminal into someone like (or superior to) the middle-class reader, *Catherine* literally downgrades the reader, forcing recognition of his or her kinship with low scoundrels. "How dreadfully like a rascal is to an honest man," the narrator comments, making explicit a connection that is implied continually. A more specific attack is directed at what lies behind public taste for Newgate fiction. This undercurrent surfaces dramatically at the end of Chapter 13 when the narrator indicts the public, "gorged with blood and foul Newgate garbage," and asks his characters to stretch their throats, "for the public is thirsty, and must have blood!" Thackeray's disgust here is linked closely to his disgust at the excitement generated by public hangings, a subject much on his mind at the time of *Catherine*. In *Catherine* itself his main characters return from the hanging of Macshane all "smiling and rosy" (ch. 8). The hint here of vampire-like activity is reinforced by the imagery in Thackeray's articles on actual hangings where he refers to the crowd indulging in "a glut of blood" and "feast of blood."[11] In this context John Ruskin's later comment on Thackeray seems particularly appropriate to his purpose in *Catherine*. "Thackeray," Ruskin complained, "settled like a meatfly on whatever one had got for dinner, and made one sick of it."[12]

Barry Lyndon and Picaresque Heroes

"The Luck of Barry Lyndon," serialized in *Fraser's Magazine* (1844) and revised and published in book form as *The Memoirs of Barry Lyndon, Esq.* (1856), is Thackeray's most significant work of fiction before *Vanity Fair*.[13] Like *Catherine* it grows out of his reaction to the popular tales of roguery and is motivated by a similar desire to convince novelists of their responsibility to represent "life as it really appears to them to be; not to foist off upon the public figures pretending to be delineations of human nature,—gay and agreeable cut-throats, otto-of-rose murderers" and other such fanciful creations (*Barry Lyndon*, pt. II, ch. 3). He sets up his hero, Redmond Barry, in deliberate contrast to "those perfect impossible heroes, whom our writers love to describe" (pt. II, ch. 1). But in *Barry Lyndon* the literary target is secondary rather than primary, for Thackeray's focus has shifted from a criticism of books to a criticism of life. He is now more interested in exploring character, especially in relation to social context, and *Barry Lyndon* represents the transformation of the parodist into the realist.

Barry Lyndon belongs to the tradition of the picaresque novel, a form characterized by its loosely structured, episodic account of a rogue's struggle to survive and succeed in a tough, usually corrupt world. To Thackeray's original readers the Irish nationality of his hero would have recalled immediately a particular type of picaresque, the Irish novel popular at the time.[14] But the most striking quality of *Barry Lyndon* then and now is its sustained irony. Thackeray has Redmond Barry tell his own story in such a way that while he justifies himself in his own eyes, he damns himself in the eyes of the reader. Thackeray had experimented with unintentionally self-revealing narrators before (Yellowplush is an example) but only in short, obvious sketches. The sheer difficulty of attempting to maintain an ironic stance consistently and clearly for the length of a whole novel made the writing of *Barry Lyndon* notably grueling.[15] Although Thackeray's control does falter on occasion, the novel fully deserves Anthony Trollope's description of it as a "remarkable" achievement.[16]

Irony serves to make Thackeray's point about the self-deception and monumental complacency of moral evil. Where in *Catherine* he emphasized its banality and sordidness, in *Barry Lyndon* he underlines its blindness and self-centeredness. Redmond Barry relates the story of a life marked by his own willful degradation of others and himself but casts himself as "a martyr to the rascality of others and a victim of my own generous and confiding temper" (pt. II, ch. 3). We do not make the mistake of believing him, for from the novel's opening paragraph he has been exposing the keynotes of his character: self-inflation, obsession with an illusory social status, and evasion of responsibility. "Since the days of Adam," Barry begins, "there has been hardly a mischief done in this world but a woman has been at the bottom of it. Ever since ours was a family (and that must be very *near* Adam's time,—so old, noble, and illustrious are the Barrys, as every body knows), women have played a mighty part with the destinies of our race."

Barry is at least correct about the central role of women in his life. His father dies when he is a child and Barry is raised in genteel poverty in rural, eighteenth-century Ireland by a pretentious, devoted mother who fills her son with tales of his noble lineage and status. He begins lying and bragging at an early age, fighting anyone who challenges the truth of his stories. Supported by his fists and his fantasies, Redmond Barry grows up vain, ignorant, violent, and naive. At fifteen (like so many Thackerayan heroes) he falls violently in love with an older woman, his cousin Nora Brady. While toying with young Barry, Nora is trying seriously to marry an Englishman whose money the Brady clan needs badly. To get rid of the wild young cousin, the family allows him to fight a duel with his rival, then deceives the boy by telling him he has killed the Englishman and must flee.

By now disillusioned with Nora, Barry leaves eagerly for Dublin and is gulled almost immediately by knaves who assume (largely as a result of Barry's own lies) that he is a wealthy young gentleman. Barry himself is furious when he discovers that he has fallen among "imposters." To avoid arrest for debt he joins the army and ends up on the Continent fighting a war he does not understand. Impersonating an officer, he escapes from the army, vowing "never again to fall from the rank of a gentleman" (pt. I, ch. 6). But soon he is an ordinary soldier again, this time in the Prussian army which he is blackmailed into "volunteering" to join. When peace is eventually declared, he goes to Berlin where he serves as a spy (among other things) for the nephew of the Minister of Police. Barry lives well but chafes at his "slavery." When his uncle, a professional gambler calling himself the Chevalier de Balibari, shows up in Berlin, Barry escapes (disguised as his uncle) with de Balibari's connivance.

The two join forces and gamble their way around the courts of Europe. Barry meets the English Countess Lyndon, a vain, foolish but rich woman whom he courts under the eye of her invalid husband. When the husband dies, Barry wins the widow, using a variety of techniques of intimidation which both repel and fascinate her. Upon their marriage he adds his wife's name to his own, becoming Barry Lyndon. He lives extravagantly and wildly, spoiling the son born to him, and tyrannizing over his wife and her son by her first husband. Eventually, Barry alienates almost everyone in his society and retires to Castle Lyndon in Ireland where his beloved son dies at the age of nine and his wife tries to escape from him. She succeeds finally, and Barry degenerates quickly, spending the last nineteen years of his life in Fleet Prison drinking himself to death, tended only by his faithful mother.

All through his narration Barry avoids confronting his own role in making his life, citing fate ("a puppet in the hands of Fate") or bad luck ("as ill luck would have it") or "that vulgar Corsican," Napoleon, who ruined the world for gentlemen. Barry's tendency mocks the general impulse of rogue literature, especially the Newgate novel, to cast the blame for the hero's wrongdoing onto some other force, usually an oppressive society. Thackeray is particularly insistent on individual moral responsibility in *Barry Lyndon* because here he does in fact show how the character of his hero is shaped by social context and external experience. To dispel any urge we may have to absolve Barry because of his early life, brutalization in the army, and so on, Thackeray has him exceed the limits of sympathy continually, so stressing that to explain is not to excuse.

Through his own words and actions, reinforced by the reactions of others, Barry is condemned consistently. And his refusal to assume responsibility for his life serves as a significant index to his radical failure as a human being.

At the same time, however, the condemnation of Redmond Barry involves not just one individual but a whole social code. In the exposure of Barry's gentlemanly code of honor Thackeray is sharpening the satiric and analytic skills that will turn him into a social novelist. Barry is reared in a system that defines a gentleman by his blood and by his skill with a sword. By his time and in his shallow eyes, the code has degenerated into a matter of externals and confusion of means with ends. The young Redmond declares grandly that a gentleman "dies, but never apologizes" (pt. I, ch. 3), and the mature Redmond asserts seriously: "What is life good for but honour? and that is so indispensable that we should attain it any how" (pt. I, ch. 11). His simple-minded pursuit of his idea of a gentleman results in blindness to reality, profound self-deception, and a thirst for revenge on and power over the genteel world that dismissed him as a young man.

Barry literally materializes the idea of honor by identifying it with physical victory. Thackeray draws specific attention to this in a note, pointing out that when Barry does something considered disreputable, he usually fights a duel and emerges victorious, "from which he argues that he is a man of undoubted honour" (pt. I, ch. 8). Such transformation of moral or spiritual values into material manifestations characterizes the entire world of the novel and is to become a constant theme in Thackeray's fiction. Novels themselves are also implicated in this process of debasement. Novels, Thackeray suggests in *Barry Lyndon,* participate in and perpetuate the moral confusion by endowing their heroes at the end with "every worldly prosperity." "Is it not a poor standard, that of the *summum bonum?*" he asks. "The greatest good in life is not to be a lord, perhaps not even to be happy" (pt. 11, ch. 1). Although Thackeray himself is not quite sure what is the "greatest good," his suspicion of prevailing definitions is to endure throughout his career. *Barry Lyndon* thus widens Thackeray's scope and establishes many of the major concerns of his fiction. But the making of the novelist is not complete until the central, more discursive analysis of society in *The Book of Snobs.*

The Book of Snobs and English Society

In February 1846 *Punch* began running Thackeray's most successful series, "The Snobs of England, by one of themselves," published in book form in 1848 as *The Book of Snobs*.[17] In the final number of the series Thackeray proclaimed: "THE NATIONAL MIND IS AWAKENED TO THE SUBJECT OF SNOBS. The word Snob has taken a place in our honest English vocabulary" ("Chapter Last"). This humorous boast is not entirely facetious. Thackeray is responsible for establishing the modern meaning of "snob," and he established it so firmly that Victorian readers could hardly avoid recognizing the pervasiveness of snobbery in their society. Before Thackeray redefined the term, *snob* meant a person of the lower class and the word was associated in particular with Cambridge University where "snob" referred contemptuously to anyone outside the university. In Thackeray's hands those who had labeled others "snobs" were now called "snobs" themselves. His celebrated definition in Chapter 2 of *The Book of Snobs* reads: "*He who meanly admires mean things is a Snob.*" But as his numerous examples illustrate, this general definition refers in practice to a special kind of meanness: the automatic evaluation of others according only to their social rank.

The old and new meanings of "snob" mingle in the opening chapter where Thackeray accomplishes his redefinition through ironic anecdote. Here the narrator, Mr. Snob, sets out to define a snob (in the old sense) by relating his sad experience with his friend, Marrowfat. Marrowfat was a highly resourceful man of "excellent heart," but Marrowfat, it turned out, ate peas with his knife. Such behavior naturally obliged Mr. Snob to end their friendship. Marrowfat, it is true, had saved his life, but "as an English gentleman, what was I to do?" In a few ironic paragraphs Thackeray has effectively displaced the traditional definition (Marrowfat as snob) and set up the new sense of the term, using his own narrator as example. Mr. Snob, of course, is not always so obtuse, and as a Snobographer he does a thorough job of cataloguing other English varieties in succeeding chapters.

He points out Military Snobs of various types and the equally diverse Club Snobs, Dining-Out Snobs and Dinner-Giving Snobs, University Snobs, Country Snobs, City Snobs, Literary Snobs, and numerous others of the species, so making good his early claim that "I have . . . an eye for a Snob" ("Prefatory Remarks"). The satire becomes especially sharp when he focuses on Fashionable Snobs, who change their name from Alfred Smith Muggins to Sir Alured Mogyns Smyth de Mogyns; on Continental Snobs, whose invincible conviction of British superiority makes the nation "magnificently hated" in Europe; and on the Snob Royal in the person of George IV (Gorgius IV), who "in the vigour of his youth" invented a shoe buckle. The institution of the aristocracy, in fact, maintains snobbery, spreading

Lordolatry through all levels of society and creating the social psychology that generates all the varieties of Snob. "How can we help Snobbishness, with such a prodigious national institution erected for its worship?" asks Mr. Snob (ch. 3). It is impossible not to be a snob in England, he insists, because snobbery infects the entire social structure: "We are sneaking and bowing and cringing on the one hand, or bullying and scorning on the other, from the lowest to the highest" ("Chapter Last").

The "we" is typical of Thackeray. He allows neither his narrative voice nor his reader to escape inclusion in the indictment. "Other satirists flatter their readers," George Henry Lewes commented in his review of *The Book of Snobs*, ". . . but [Thackeray] ruthlessly arrests the complacent chuckle, and turns the laugh against the laugher."[18] One such "ruthless arrest" concludes the chapter on the bloated Snob Royal, George IV: "If you want to moralise upon the mutability of human affairs, go and see the figure of Gorgius in his real, identical robes, at the waxwork.—Admittance one shilling. Children and flunkeys sixpence. Go, and pay sixpence" (ch. 2). Thackeray can deliver such a savage punch without alienating the reader because he never forgets that he too is a flunkey. "Whenever he sneers," G.K. Chesterton has noted, "it is at his own potential self. When he rebukes, he knows it is self-rebuke." In contrast to Charles Dickens, for example, whose narrator castigates and declaims from a moral position above the reader (and the characters), Thackeray's narrator typically identifies with the reader's world and so establishes a bond that allows a different kind of moral persuasion from that of Dickens. Dickens and other Victorians might have planned a Book of Snobs, Chesterton adds, but "it was Thackeray, and Thackeray alone, who wrote the great subtitle, 'By One of Themselves.'"[19]

Thackeray's analysis of the nature of English society in *The Book of Snobs* is sweeping and devastating, providing him with a framework for the social vision of *Vanity Fair*. But it is the criticism of a reformer, not a radical. Despite occasional outbursts, Thackeray does not advocate a complete reorganization of society and an end to all social difference. He sees difference as inevitable; what he wants to change are the grounds of difference. Action and character should be the grounds of evaluation and not hereditary rank or money. The argument is more moral than political, urging a change in values rather than a change in social structure. To focus the change, Thackeray sets up his concept of the gentleman, providing a lengthy, tentative definition in which words like "honest," "generous," "gentle," and "brave" figure prominently. The gentleman, as Thackeray presents him in *The Book of Snobs*, possesses in particular the domestic virtues, paying his bills and conducting himself as "a loyal son, a true husband, and honest father" (ch. 2). Redmond Barry, of course, would dismiss this contemptuously as the description of a grocer, and Gordon Ray has argued that it is precisely because Thackeray expanded the gentlemanly ideal "to fit a middle-class rather than aristocratic context" that he was so successful with the middle-class Victorian public.[20] Certainly, *The Book of Snobs* appealed to that public, despite its puncturing of the snobbery of "the respectable classes."

With this work Thackeray's literary apprenticeship was over. He had exposed shams, tested techniques, explored alternatives, and was now ready to build the insights garnered in his decade of experience into a major novel.

"Becky's second appearance in the character of Clytemnestra." *Vanity Fair,* Ch. 67

Chapter Three
"The Sentiment of Reality": *Vanity Fair*
Publication and Reception

Unlike Thackeray's earlier fiction, *Vanity Fair* appeared in independent monthly parts, a form of publication popularized by Charles Dickens.[1] Each month from January 1847 to July 1848 a thirty-two-page, yellow-covered installment went on sale for one shilling, competing on the stands with the famous greenish-blue cover of Dickens, whose *Dombey and Son* was appearing at the same time. Each month Thackeray raced to meet the deadline for copy, complaining that the "printer's devil" was "always hanging about the premises" (*Letters*, 2:381).

The monthly pressure was especially intense for Thackeray because he not only wrote but also illustrated his novel, the only major Victorian novelist to do so.[2] *Vanity Fair* is illustrated profusely with full-page engravings, smaller dropped-in woodcuts, and pictorial capitals. Although Thackeray did not rate his drawings highly (calling them "tenth or twentieth rate performances"), he used them skillfully to supplement, interpret, and sometimes add to the text.[3] In the final chapter of the novel, for example, an illustration provides information not given in the text. Dobbin talks to Jos Sedley who wants to leave Becky Sharp but is terrified that "she'd kill me if she knew it." The reader is likely to dismiss his fear were it not for the illustration which shows Becky behind a curtain listening to the conversation. The text makes no mention of her presence, but the drawing casts a sinister light on Jos's death three months later and renders more intelligible the rumors that Becky killed him. The illustrations as a whole reinforce a negative interpretation of Becky who appears in them as unchangingly sly and unattractive, while Dobbin in contrast changes from a gawky adolescent to a handsome man.

Serial publication meant that the novelist had to structure his novel in terms of the monthly unit, making sure that each number worked effectively to satisfy and yet intrigue the reader. Under this system the impact of the public on novels was often direct and immediate. So Dickens, noting the sagging sales of *Martin Chuzzlewit,* sent his hero to America in an effort to boost circulation, and Thackeray concluded *The Newcomes* with a marriage he did not believe in because "what could a fellow do? So many people wanted 'em married" (*Letters,* 3:465n). Aside from such direct response to the market, serial publication encouraged the use of subplots to diversify and maintain interest. In the hands of masters of the serial form like Thackeray and Dickens, the multiple plots allowed a deepening of thematic exploration through parallel and contrast, as with the stories of Becky and Amelia or Becky and Dobbin in *Vanity Fair.*[4]

In addition, some of the most telling effects of Victorian fiction grow directly out of the form of publication. Two of the most memorable moments in *Vanity Fair,* for instance, were originally endings of a monthly part. Number 4 ended with one of the most famous lines in the English novel, Becky's surprise response to Sir Pitt's proposal: "Oh, Sir—I—I'm *married already*" (ch. 14). For the next month Victorian readers were left to speculate about the identity of the mysterious husband. Number 9 concluded with the shock of George Osborne's death at Waterloo: "and Amelia was praying for George, who was lying on his face, dead, with a bullet through his heart" (ch. 32). In the next number Thackeray switched to Brighton and Miss Crawley, thereby making a point as well as prolonging the reader's suspense.

Partly as a result of such exploitation of the form, fictional characters tended to become very real to Victorian readers who debated their behavior continually both in private and in the reviews. In the prologue to *Vanity Fair* (written after the novel was completed) Thackeray indicates the general reaction when he notes that the "famous little Becky Puppet has been pronounced to be uncommonly flexible in the joints, and lively on the wire," while "the Amelia Doll . . . has had a smaller circle of admirers" ("Before the Curtain"). Even as they responded to Becky's vitality, however, Victorian readers did not (like some modern readers) lose sight of her corruption; nor, on the other hand, did they melt automatically at the pathos of Amelia. The *Spectator's* reaction is typical: "*Vanity Fair* is said by its author to be a novel without a hero: which is undoubtedly a truth; but the heroines do not make up for this omission, since one is without a heart, and the other without a head."[5]

Two motifs recur in the reviews of *Vanity Fair*: praise for its realism and dismay at its depressing picture of life. These two qualities in the novel are interrelated, as Elizabeth Rigby noted shrewdly in the *Quarterly Review*: "It is this reality which is at once the charm and misery here."[6] Thackeray's contemporaries testify to how deeply *Vanity Fair* struck its first readers as a new kind of fiction remarkable for its fidelity to actual experience. Wanting to articulate their sense of how it differed from the conventional novels of the time, they relied on phrases like "life-like," "life as it is," and "literal photograph." But most also agreed with Robert Bell of *Fraser's* who found Thackeray's picture of society "true" but not "the whole truth." Thackeray was often accused of cynicism, extremism, and of somehow being unhealthy. Invoking an image that we find repeated in the reviews, Bell referred to the novel's "foul atmosphere," to its "stifling" quality which made the reader pant for fresh or clear air.[7] Thackeray seems to have been struck by this imagery and included it in his often-quoted reply to Bell: "If I had put in more fresh air as you call it my object would have been defeated—It is to indicate, in cheerful terms, that we are for the most part an abominably foolish and selfish people 'desperately wicked' and all eager after vanities. . . . I want to leave everybody dissatisfied and unhappy at the end of the story—we ought all to be with our own and all other stories" (*Letters*, 2:423). The Victorian imagery of heavy or stifling air captures the undefinable way in which *Vanity Fair* generates the profound and vague dissatisfaction with life to which Thackeray refers here. Life in *Vanity Fair* is soiled. It is this that the imagery of air intuitively expresses, as G. K. Chesterton knew when he remarked that there is "something which haunts the air and discolours the very scenery of Vanity Fair."[8]

The Idea of Vanity

When Thackeray hit on *Vanity Fair* as his title (replacing the original "The Novel Without a Hero"), he found an image and focus that turned his satiric sketches into an integrated vision of English society. The image comes from John Bunyan's allegory, *The Pilgrim's Progress* (1678), where Christian and Evangelist must pass through "a Town called Vanity" on their way to the Celestial City. This town holds a "lusty fair" all year round called Vanity Fair: "at this fair are all such merchandise sold, as houses, lands, trades, places, honours, preferments, titles, countries, kingdoms, lusts, pleasures, and delights of all sorts, as whores, bawds, wives, husbands, children, masters, servants, lives, blood, bodies, souls, silver, gold, pearls, precious stones, and what not."[9] With its debasement of all things into "merchandise," Bunyan's fair mirrors Thackeray's world where money is the prime motive for action and relationship. Both Bunyan and Thackeray use the word "vanity" in its biblical sense, drawing on Ecclesiastes and its well-known statement: "Vanity of vanities, Saith the Preacher; all is vanity." For Thackeray the phrase is to become a persistent reference in all his novels whenever he ponders the futility or emptiness of human goals. We are "all eager after vanities," as he told Robert Bell. The Latin root, *vanus,* meaning "empty" helps to locate Thackeray's use of the word and to remind us of its link to ideas of insubstantiality and nothing-ness. The more specialized modern sense of vanity as overvaluation of personal appearance is just one particular form of vanity, represented most clearly in Thackeray's novel by the handsome George Osborne cut down on the field of Waterloo.

The idea of vanity would clearly appeal to Thackeray with his early and continuing interest in shams, fakes, illusions, and with his melancholy sense of life. But for all its seriousness and incisiveness in exposing cultural values, *Vanity Fair* is a comic masterpiece exhibiting comedy's joy in the sheer vitality and resilience of life. It opens with the celebrated scene of Becky Sharp, released from Miss Pinkerton's academy for young ladies, tossing out the window the symbol of oppressive authority, Samuel Johnson's *Dictionary.* The moment expresses not only Becky's defiance but the novel's delight in the energies of life exploding the institutions that would contain them. The irrepressible Becky is on her way. Orphaned daughter of a dissolute artist and a French opera-girl, she belongs to no class and has no family connections to support her. Ambitious, intelligent, and unscrupulous, Becky knows that an advantageous marriage is the surest way to security and status, and to that end she becomes an expert actress, acting out the female roles expected by men of her time. So when she meets the eligible, fat, and timid Jos Sedley, she makes "a respectful virgin-like curtsey" and modestly keeps her "large, odd, and attractive" eyes lowered.

Jos is the brother of Becky's friend, Amelia Sedley, and what Becky pretends to be the blushing Amelia actually is. A product of her weal-thy middle-class background, Amelia is conventional, naive, and sentimental, thoroughly taken in by Becky's pretended innocence and genuinely moved by her playing of the role of friendless orphan. Though eager for Becky to succeed in marrying Jos, Amelia is absorbed in her own love for the handsome and vain George Osborne. An Army officer trying to forget his commercial roots, the snobbish George is appalled at the idea of a nobody like Becky marrying into the family that he plans (eventually) to join, and he engineers the comic anticlimax of the Jos and Becky affair. Working on Jos's fears and insecurities, he so embarrasses the portly suitor that Jos flees the field. Defeated, Becky leaves the Sedley house to take up a post as governess at the country seat of Sir Pitt Crawley.

As the focus shifts to the aristocracy, the social comedy darkens. Sir Pitt is illiterate and boorish, an old reprobate who abuses his wife (soon dead) and lusts after Becky. Of his two sons, the heir (also Pitt) is a cold and pious humbug, while the younger Rawdon, captain in the Life Guards, is an inarticulate brawler with a reputation for drinking, dueling, and womanizing. Sir Pitt's brother, the Reverend Bute Crawley, prefers country sports to sermons; indeed, his sermons are written by his calculating wife who struggles to maintain the appearance of gentility in the face of constant debts. Like most of the Crawleys, Mrs. Bute Crawley cultivates and flatters the rich Miss Crawley, sister to Sir Pitt, in the hope of inheriting some and preferably all of her seventy thousand pounds. The current favorite in the inheritance race is Rawdon whose spirit Miss Crawley professes to like. Becky soon makes herself indispensable to Sir Pitt and then moves on to do the same with Miss Crawley. In the expectation of his large legacy, she secretly marries Rawdon and is stunned when the unknowing old Sir Pitt hobbles up to London to throw himself at her feet and proposes marriage. Forced to confess that she is married already, Becky "wept some of the most genuine tears that ever fell from her eyes" (ch. 14).

When Miss Crawley discovers the marriage, she turns against her two former favorites, and Mrs. Bute Crawley rushes in eagerly to fill the void left by Becky and Rawdon. But her rigidity finally alienates the old lady who then turns to the gentle fiancée of the younger Pitt, Lady Jane. Despite the failure of her repeated attempts at reconciliation with Miss Crawley, Becky remains hopeful and her spirits are high when she reencounters her friend, Amelia, lately married to George Osborne. Amelia's marriage, much like that of Becky, has created family schisms and undermined financial expectations. George is now alienated from his father who forbad the match he had himself arranged when the Sedleys, his old friends, fell into bankruptcy. George himself, in fact, had not been eager to marry Amelia but was persuaded to do so by William Dobbin, whose own long and silent love for Amelia no one (including Amelia) notices.

Shortly after their marriage, England declares war against Napoleon, and all the main characters travel to Brussels. In the city the mood is festive, but Amelia is made miserable by Becky's flirtation with George and by his obvious attraction to her. At the famous ball on the night before the battle of Waterloo, Amelia pines while Becky glitters. George slips Becky a note proposing that they run away together but is called to battle before she can respond. While the soldiers fight, contradictory rumors fly around Brussels; and in one of the novel's most brilliant impressionistic sequences, Thackeray captures the effect of war on the civilian population, the complex mixture of fear, confusion, greed, loyalty, and betrayal that it engenders. Against a background of commotion and the constant sound of cannon, he highlights the comedy of the blustering Jos Sedley in a panic, the pathos of Amelia's anguished fear for George, the anti-romance of Becky's cool preparations for survival. When silence falls, George is dead.

After Waterloo, Becky and Rawdon live well for some years in Paris by spreading rumors that they will soon inherit a large sum from Miss Crawley. Becky gives birth to a son whom she ignores but whom his father, an increasingly sympathetic figure, loves deeply. Decamping from Paris without paying their bills, they move to London where they continue to live well purely on credit and where Becky is befriended by Lord Steyne, one of the highest nobles in the land. Exhilarated by the society to which this witty and degenerate aristocrat introduces her, she neglects Rawdon, moving from one social triumph to another. Matters come to a head when Rawdon is arrested for debt in circumstances which suggest Lord Steyne's connivance. Rawdon writes to Becky, asking her to free him, and she affects concern but manages not to bail him out, leaving his sister-in-law, Lady Jane, to effect Rawdon's release. Rawdon returns home to discover Becky, resplendent in diamonds, entertaining Steyne. He erupts, tearing off her diamonds and knocking down the nobleman whose forehead he scars for life with a diamond brooch that he flings at him. When Rawdon discovers that Becky has been hiding away considerable funds, his disillusion is complete. He leaves Becky, gives his son into the care of Lady Jane and her husband (now Sir Pitt), and accepts a post as governor of Coventry Island, a virtual death sentence at the time.

While Becky has been playing high society games, the widowed Amelia has been living in obscurity with her bankrupt parents, suffering a broken father, a nagging mother, and the constant meannesses of poverty. Her one consolation—her obsession, in fact—is her son, Georgy, whom her overwhelming love threatens to turn into as vain and self-centered a creature as his father, now transformed by Amelia's memory into a perfect husband and hero. The faithful Dobbin, a major in India, continues to love without return, his many kindnesses unknown or unappreciated. Pressure increases on Amelia when Georgy's grandfather, old Osborne, unable to forgive Amelia but yearning after his grandson, proposes to bring up the boy as his heir, allowing him to see his mother occasionally. Unable to bear such separation, Amelia refuses until the financial situation of the Sedleys becomes so desperate that she agrees to the "treaty of capitulation." Spoiled by his doting grandfather, Georgy becomes ever more imperious and patronizing, but his character is rescued by the return of Dobbin who cures him of the worst of his excesses. With Dobbin returns Jos, a wealthy man, and the family's fortunes improve rapidly as he settles his sister and father (the mother having died) into a comfortable home. Dobbin declares his love to Amelia but she clings to the memory of George and to her idea of fidelity, and he must settle for a brotherly relationship. Amelia's father dies and soon thereafter so does old Osborne, whose will leaves Amelia an annuity as well as the promised legacy for Georgy. With news of the will, Amelia's social standing rises dramatically, but she tires of the society that had ignored her in her days of desperation and welcomes the idea of a Continental holiday with Dobbin, Jos, and her son.

In the German town of Pumpernickel they run into Becky Sharp, calling herself Madame de Raudon and leading a rather dubious life. In the years since Rawdon left, she has moved about Europe, her sporadic attempts at respectability gradually ceasing as she becomes "a vagabond," drifting into a world of boarding houses and gambling tables, rouge and brandy. Becky enjoys the bohemian life, particularly in Pumpernickel where she lives among pedlars, circus tumblers, and students. But when Jos Sedley reappears, she again sets out to capture him and once more he succumbs. Amelia also recovers the sympathy for Becky that she had lost, but Dobbin warns her against the association, hinting at the flirtation with George. The hint is fatal. Amelia rises up and attacks Dobbin, but he finally can stand no more. After eighteen years he recognizes that he has wasted his emotions on a woman incapable of feeling "such an attachment as mine deserves to mate with." Announcing that "I have spent enough of my life at this play," Dobbin leaves (ch. 66).

Amelia finds herself disconcerted and unhappy. Finally, she writes to Dobbin just before Becky urges her to give up her foolish allegiance to George, revealing that George was but a "padded booby" who made love to Becky a week after his marriage. Dobbin and Amelia marry, but Dobbin's love has lost its intensity and its illusions even as it retains its kindness. Becky sticks to Jos who becomes terrified of her and whom (it is rumored) she kills for a share of his insurance money. She returns to England where her son, now Sir Rawdon Crawley, gives her a liberal allowance but refuses to see her. Eminently respectable, Becky presents herself as an injured woman, attends church and supports charities, her shift in role reflecting the increasing social importance of the Evangelical middle class after the Napoleonic Wars. Always alert to social currents, Becky has recognized the waning of aristocratic influence and attached herself to the emerging powers. In the last scene of the novel she stands behind a booth at a charity fair, signaling the new hypocrisy, the latest sham to gain currency in Vanity Fair.

Vanity Fair extends the analysis of the false and the hollow begun in Thackeray's early work and focused in *The Book of Snobs*. The novel is crowded with snobs of all sorts, from Irish Snobs (Mrs. O'Dowd) to Clerical Snobs (the Bute Crawleys) to Academic Snobs (Miss Pinkerton). But Military and City Snobs receive the most extended exposure through the portrayal of George Osborne and his father, old Osborne. George's aristocratic army acquaintances delight the middle-class old Osborne who drops names and preens in his own circle. In the presence of an aristocrat, however, "he grovelled before him and my-lorded him as only a free-born Briton can do" (ch. 13). The equally snobbish son is used and ridiculed by impoverished aristocrats who recognize that George would "go to the deuce to be seen with a lord" (ch. 14). Rawdon Crawley makes this observation, and Rawdon represents the false gentlemanly ideal which so impresses George. Like Redmond Barry, Rawdon Crawley (in the early part of the novel) stands for an outmoded and vicious idea of the gentleman. Rawdon is a "blood," a fashionable man about town, adept at rat-hunting, drinking, gambling, and piling up debts. As a man of action, he finds language rather beyond him: "Jove—aw—Gad—aw—it's the finest segaw I ever smoked in the world aw" (ch. 11).

In their pursuit of social status and money the inhabitants of Vanity Fair create a distorted value system. Love is equated with money, as in the statement that Miss Crawley "had a balance at her banker's which would have made her beloved anywhere" (ch. 9). Marriage becomes a mercenary pursuit and calculated game for self-enrichment. So Mrs. Bute "played for Bute and won him at Harrowgate" (ch. 11), while the unhappy Lady Steyne is more brutally "sold" to Lord Steyne (ch. 47). Moral terms have only a financial meaning to old Osborne, who tells young George after the death of his impoverished old friend, Sedley: "And yet he was a better man than I was, this day twenty years—a better man I should say by ten thousand pound" (ch. 61). For Becky moral ruin is primarily economic disaster: "All her lies and her schemes, all her selfishness and her wiles, all her wit and genius had come to this bankruptcy" (ch. 53). But the "bankruptcy" of Becky, sitting alone with "a heap of tumbled vanities" about her, is clearly more than financial, and her story underlines not just the moral confusion of her world but also its emptiness. As Lord Steyne recognizes from his position at the top of Vanity Fair: "Everybody is striving for what is not worth the having" (ch. 48).

Vanity Fair defines nineteenth-century society as not only immoral but fundamentally hollow. Comically, through titles like Lady Bareacres and His Transparency the Duke, and more poignantly through figures like the "puffy" Jos Sedley who dresses with enormous care to "dine with nobody," Thackeray conveys the sense of a world without substance, its solid appearance disguising an inner void. It stands precariously, supported by a tottering "pillar of the state" like Sir Pitt, while the "tall carved portals" of great houses like Gaunt House belie the sterility and madness within. In a passage that captures the almost surreal unreality of this world, the narrator reports that the mad younger son of Lord Steyne "was gazetted to Brazil. But people knew better; he never returned from that Brazil expedition—never died there—never lived there—never was there at all. He was nowhere: he was gone out altogether" (ch. 47). "Brazil," the gossips insinuate, is actually an insane asylum.[10]

Gossip is central to *Vanity Fair* and to its theme of unreality. As has often been noticed, Thackeray's narrative mode itself resembles that of gossip.[11] The narrator relies on gossips like Tom Eaves for information and reports constantly what "the world" said of so-and-so. Moreover, his own style with its intimate tone, hints, unfinished sentences, and trailing speculations mimics the manner of gossip. All this works to underline the elusive and insubstantial nature of what constitutes reality for those in Vanity Fair. Characters in the book tend to exist through rumor; as a result, their actual reality becomes obscure and ineffective, while the insubstantial language of rumor becomes "a moving force and therefore a reality."[12] In this way Becky and Rawdon can "live well on nothing a year" for several years solely on the basis of reputation and rumor. Mrs. Bute Crawley exhibits a similar reliance on the power of suggestion when she dresses her daughters so well for the marriage market that "it began almost to be believed that the four sisters had had fortunes left them by their aunt" (ch. 39). The narrator calls this behavior "lying," and in Vanity Fair lies dominate. Its very language becomes deceptive, for this world has "no particular objection to vice, but an insuperable repugnance to hearing vice called by its proper name" (ch. 64). Reality is hidden or ignored as the creation of false appearance becomes the norm and the central "fact" of existence. So Becky's "happier days" are not days of innocence but days "when she was not innocent, but not found out" (ch. 64).

To live in this way creates an intolerable strain. Even Becky, hustling her way through the bustling fair with apparently inexhaustible energy, reveals a face "haggard, weary, and terrible" when she is alone. As soon as Rawdon awakens, however, the mask is back in place and she greets him with "fresh candid smiles" (ch. 52). Her behavior is symptomatic. After the flare, the noise, and the gaiety of the fair, the narrator remarks, we are all equally "miserable in private" (ch. 19). Direct comment is reinforced by symbols and images that suggest the quiet desperation underlying most lives in Vanity Fair. The most memorable of these is Jane Osborne sitting in an empty drawing room near a loudly ticking clock: "The great glass over the mantel-piece, faced by the other great console glass at the opposite end of the room, increased and multiplied between them the brown Holland bag in which the chandelier hung; until you saw these brown Holland bags fading away in endless perspectives, and this apartment of Miss Osborne's seemed the centre of a system of drawing-rooms" (ch. 42). In the silence broken only by the ticking clock, in the mirrors, the covered chandelier, and the endless repetition, Thackeray embodies powerfully the emptiness at the heart of Vanity Fair.

The Narrator of *Vanity Fair*

In the Preface to *Pendennis* Thackeray defined a novel as "a sort of confidential talk between writer and reader," and some readers of *Vanity Fair* have complained that there is rather too much of this talk in the novel. Certainly, the narrator dominates to a degree unusual even in Victorian fiction. Furthermore, his voice is puzzling as well as intrusive, playing now the fool, now the preacher, now the man of the world, now the man of sentiment. His age changes and he never seems to be quite sure about his marital status. Suddenly he appears in Pumpernickel where he meets the characters. Whereas other Victorian narrators (like those of George Eliot, for instance) reassure and guide the reader, Thackeray's slippery character keeps us off-balance and uncertain. And that is the whole point. Through the narrator Thackeray turns reading from a passive into an active process, so furthering his campaign for realism by bringing closer together the experience of reading and the experience of living.[13]

Thackeray's narrator is distinguished by his conversational, personal tone. Dickens usually assumes a public, oratorical voice; George Eliot creates a detached analyst; and even Fielding (whom Thackeray occasionally resembles) adopts a more impersonal role. But the informal style of *Vanity Fair* puts us in a more private, familiar world where the narrator can respond to his characters and to his hypothetical reader in a more casual

and intimate fashion. Thackeray presents his narrator in the prologue as
Manager of the Performance, and in one of the novel's more formal
moments the narrator asks leave "as a man and a brother" not only to
introduce his characters but "to step down from the platform, and talk
about them" (ch. 8). The novel as a whole takes place down here, away
from the platform with its implied superiority and detachment. The effect
of the narrator's highly personal tone, as Juliet McMaster has pointed out,
is to make the reader react personally both to the narrator and to the
characters; and this in turn animates the fiction. The narrator's fallible
commentary provokes our own response to the characters. By so responding, we endow them with a life resembling that of real people and turn
their world into one "that has somehow overlapped with [our] own."[14]

This overlapping is also managed more directly by the frequent breaking of dramatic illusion when the narrator moves out of the fictional world
into the world of the reader. After introducing the rich Miss Crawley, for
example, he proceeds to generalize: "What a dignity it gives an old lady,
that balance at the banker's!" To ensure recognition of the relevance of this
irony to actuality, he involves the reader, creating an elaborate hypothesis
about "your" life: "Your wife" and "your little girls" work busily to please
the wealthy relative. "You yourself, dear sir, forget to go to sleep after
dinner. . . . Is it so, or is it not so? I appeal to the middle classes."
Characteristically, the narrator himself is not immune: "Ah, gracious
powers! I wish you would send me an old aunt" (ch. 9). Moments like
these break down the barrier between fiction and life, asserting a parallel
between the narrative and our own lives. Fiction is no longer another
reality but a way back to this one, provoking self-confrontation. *Vanity
Fair* thus continues and refines the technique developed in *Catherine* of
puncturing complacency and of making the reader as much the subject of
the fiction as the characters. Its ever-changing narrative roles demand
constant alertness, trapping the reader into a response only to reveal its
inadequacy. *"Vanity Fair,"* A. E. Dyson has written, "is surely one of the
world's most devious novels."[15] And so it is. But it is also oddly
straightforward in its fusing of technique and theme. In a novel about the
vanity of the world all wear the fool's garb of motley shown on the original
cover: narrator, characters, reader.

"The Sentiment of Reality"

Thackeray's manipulation of narrator and reader is only one form of the
probing and testing that mark *Vanity Fair*. Following the tendency of his
early work, he continues the scrutiny of popular fiction and defines himself

through dissociation from it. In his overriding concern with the responsibility of the novel to reflect ordinary reality, Thackeray regarded other effects in novels as irresponsible fakery. "The Art of Novels *is* to represent Nature," he wrote in 1851, "to convey as strongly as possible the sentiment of reality—in a tragedy or a poem or a lofty drama you aim at producing different emotions; the figures moving and their words sounding heroically: but in a drawing-room drama a coat is a coat and a poker a poker; and must be nothing else according to my ethics, not an embroidered tunic, nor a great red-hot instrument like the Pantomime weapon" (*Letters,* 2:772–73). Hence his "Novel Without a Hero" and his insistence on the drawing-room drama that he is writing in the opening to Chapter 6: "I know that the tune I am piping is a very mild one," he begins and urges the reader to remember that his subject is "common life." After imagining his story rewritten in the genteel manner (Lady Amelia) or the Newgate mode (Amelia kidnapped by burglars), he advises readers to "hope for no such romance, only a homely story" (ch. 6).

As a strategy for establishing the realism of one's own novel, this anti-romance technique is as old and venerable as one of Thackeray's favorite stories, *Don Quixote.* Just as Cervantes not only showed that life is not a chivalric romance but also questioned the very value of chivalry, so Thackeray questions the assumptions behind conventions of his time. Dobbin's love for Amelia, as Jack Rawlins notes, "sensibly suggests that he who falls in love at first sight falls in love with superficialities."[16] Through inversion, distortion, or reinterpretation of conventional patterns Thackeray pursues both a criticism of his culture and an exploration of its reality. Becky is a mistreated orphan, befriended by a wealthy family, whose romance with an eligible bachelor is ruined by snobbery. Such a summary, accurate enough, only serves to point up the divergence between life in romances and life in Vanity Fair.

More complex is the introduction of Dobbin, the despised boy who nobly defends a snob (who had insulted him) against the school bully and wins, gaining esteem and popularity.[17] Although the traditional pattern is completed, the episode defines less Dobbin's heroism than his increase in folly. After the fight Dobbin "flung himself down at little Osborne's feet" to become "his valet, his dog." George Osborne remains unshaken in his snobbery, and Dobbin's homage just compounds his already formidable self-esteem. The bully, Cuff, retrieves his power by the brilliant ploy of behaving exactly like a storybook hero, while the other boys continue with the same values they had before (ch. 5).

A similar disenchantment marks more major episodes as well, most notably the Waterloo chapters where Thackeray refuses to describe the famous battle: "We do not claim to rank among the military novelists. Our place is with the non-combatants" (ch. 30). From the perspective of the non-combatants the military glory celebrated by "bards and romances" looks rather more shoddy and more horrible. Wars in general are reduced to "alternations of successful and unsuccessful murder" (ch. 32). Once again Thackeray plays out conventional patterns—the dashing young soldier dying bravely on the field, leaving a faithful wife and unborn son—but Thackeray's replay strips George's death and Amelia's widowhood of their romance. The mystique of war and death, captured in George's thrill at "the great game of war," comes down to the blunt image of Amelia's husband "lying on his face, dead, with a bullet through his heart" (ch. 32). By such playing with and against convention, by direct involvement of the reader, and by the use of profuse concrete detail, Thackeray creates in *Vanity Fair* the richly layered "sentiment of reality" which he felt it the novel's responsibility to express.

The Progress of Becky Sharp

Becky stands at the center of the satiric impulse in *Vanity Fair.* Like Redmond Barry, she functions in the picaresque tradition of the lower-class rogue fighting for social success. By tracing the progress of the rogue up the social ladder, the picaresque is particularly suited to a large-scale satire of social values, and Becky's career takes her into the different spheres of the bourgeois, the aristocrat, the bohemian. The world of satire is generally peopled by knaves and fools, and this is how Becky habitually sees her world, beginning with Miss Pinkerton's school where she recognizes (and combats) the deviousness of Miss Pinkerton and dismisses with contempt the generous folly of Miss Jemima. "I have brains," Becky thinks at one point, "and almost all the rest of the world are fools" (ch. 41). Becky stands out in *Vanity Fair* because of her zest, wit, resourcefulness, and ability to see through the masquerade. She is the source of energy in the book, and Thackeray clearly enjoys manipulating his "little Becky Puppet."

Becky becomes the vehicle of the satire, especially in the early part of the novel, where she exposes and deflates the vanity of others. Despite her own fakery, she retains the support of the reader because most of her conflicts involve despicable characters and our indignation is directed toward them rather than toward Becky. Her early victories offer a sense of release and justice, as in her skillful "routing" of George Osborne which begins with a simple gesture. George "walked up to Rebecca with a patronising, easy swagger. He was going to be kind to her and protect her.

He would even shake hands with her, as a friend of Amelia's; and saying, 'Ah, Miss Sharp! how-dy-doo?' held out his left hand towards her, expecting that she would be quite confounded at the honour." The next paragraph begins Becky's rout. "Miss Sharp put out her right fore-finger, and gave him a little nod, so cool and killing" that George is completely taken aback. From this moment his discomfort only grows as Becky turns the tables on George and proceeds to patronize him (ch. 14). In such scenes Becky is an ally of the author, furthering his puncturing of vanity.

But she is also a satiric target herself, taking her place alongside George, Jos, Miss Crawley, and the other citizens of Vanity Fair. She shares their worldliness and narrow vision: "I think I could be a good woman if I had five thousand a year" (ch. 41). And in the terms of Vanity Fair, as the narrator points out, she probably could, for Becky is the embodiment of this world. Thackeray keeps firmly in sight her ruthless self-centeredness, placing her early among the "Faithless, Hopeless, Charityless" inhabitants of the Fair (ch. 8). As the novel progresses, Becky's destructiveness becomes increasingly apparent, summed up in the famous mermaid image of Chapter 64. The image grows out of the narrator's ironic defense of himself before the squeamish "polite public" which recoils from a frank description of "vice," more particularly from frank sexuality: "Has he [the author] once forgotten the laws of politeness, and showed the monster's hideous tail above water?" Subsequent glimpses of the siren "down among the dead men" go beyond a conventional Victorian linking of sex and death to suggest the fundamental deathliness of Becky's life. Below water the sirens appear, "flapping amongst bones, or curling round corpses," and are identified as cannibals, "revelling and feasting on their wretched pickled victims" (ch. 64). Thackeray's "hint," as Charlotte Brontë noted, "is more vivid than other men's elaborate explanations."[18]

This double function of Becky points to that complexity of role that has led to so much critical controversy about her character and about Thackeray's attitude to her. Is Becky a victim or a villain? Does Thackeray intuitively support her antisocial behavior but feel obliged by Victorian convention to condemn his heroine? Does he perhaps fear her amoral (or immoral) energy?[19] The difficulty of such questions is compounded by the fact that Becky exists as a novelistic character in addition to her function in the satiric purpose of the book. Thackeray is as much interested in exploring the psychology of Vanity Fair (a novelistic enterprise) as he is intent on exposing its vice and folly. And here again Becky serves to typify her world where satisfaction and desire are marked by transience. She is a split character doomed to a profound internal restlessness. On the one hand, Becky is a rebel against the genteel world. She finds the "rigid formality" of Miss Pinkerton's suffocating, its regularity of routine oppressive, and she recalls with nostalgia the "freedom and beggary" of her childhood with her artist father (ch. 1). The tension explodes in her hurling of Johnson's *Dictionary* and in her defiant cry of "*Vive Napoleon.*" This chafing at restriction and order persists. After her fall, Becky tries "with all her might to be respectable," but "the life of humdrum virtue grew utterly tedious to her before long" (ch. 64).

Becky craves excitement and movement; at the same time, she genuinely wants security and recognition by the respectable world. Despite her flashes of rebellion, she basically accepts the existing social structure. But the incompatibility of her "wild, roving nature" and her desire to "enjoy a character for virtue" ensures that she will never be able to achieve contentment. When she fulfills her ambition of entering aristocratic society, she is bored ("yawning in spirit") and wishes she were a parson's wife or a sergeant's lady or a carnival dancer (ch. 51). It may even be that she unconsciously wills her downfall because she cannot endure stasis and must keep moving in order to stave off a frightening sense of emptiness. We leave her at the end of the book in a respectable position, but Becky's whole characterization implies that this is unlikely to be permanent and so introduces a note of instability into the conclusion. Thackeray himself reinforces this suspicion in a letter he wrote shortly before the novel completed its serial run. To an account of what happened to his characters, he added a comic P.S. announcing that news had just arrived of the failure of the Indian bank that provided Becky with her money (*Letters,* 2:377).

The Romance of Amelia Sedley

Through Becky Sharp Thackeray explores the public, social possibilities of Vanity Fair; through Amelia Sedley he investigates its private, individual possibilities. Where Becky belongs to the world of picaresque with its emphasis on success, Amelia belongs to the world of romance where feeling is the primary value. Becky's way of life ends in "bankruptcy," but Amelia's alternative is hardly more satisfying.[20] Under scrutiny, the way of romance turns out to be as disappointing as most things in Vanity Fair.

Although Amelia is meek and passive where Becky is aggressive, in her own fashion she is as self-centered as Becky, totally wrapped up in her emotion for George. War rages "all over Europe," but Amelia thinks only of George and of her own relationship with him: "The fate of Europe was Lieutenant George Osborne to her" (ch. 12). Thoroughly conventional, she forms her ideas about men and love from sentimental romances and wastes her emotion on the worthless George who reminds her of a "fairy prince." Amelia "had never seen a man so beautiful or so clever: such a figure on horseback: such a dancer: such a hero in general" (ch. 12). A. E. Dyson is surely right to remind us that "if there is a sensualist in the book, Amelia rather than Becky fills the role."[21] She dismisses Dobbin because he is "very plain and homely-looking, and exceedingly awkward and ungainly" (ch. 25). Dazzled by George's looks and manner, she overlooks the true gentleman for the sham—and pays the price. In taking his conventional heroine beyond her marriage to the conventional hero Thackeray questions the assumptions behind the typical romance and widens the range of the novel. "As his hero and heroine pass the matrimonial barrier," the narrator comments, "the novelist generally drops the curtain, as if the drama were over then" (ch. 26).

But Thackeray's drama has barely begun, and Amelia soon suffers disillusionment and unhappiness as she learns that there is a difference between storybook heroes and husbands. Nine days after her marriage she wishes she were back in her virginal white bed, with her mother "smiling over her in the morning" (ch. 26). Throughout her brief marriage Amelia suffers passively but deeply and her pain at George's departure provides one of the most powerful scenes in the novel. In a white dress, her dark hair loose, she silently follows her husband back and forth, holding a crimson sash "like a large stain of blood" against her. Her eyes are "fixed and without light" as she stands in "helpless, speechless misery" (ch. 30). The image is compelling, moving, and ominous, prefiguring the neurotic attachment that is to distort both her life and that of Dobbin.[22]

The history of Amelia as widow and Dobbin as devoted lover constitutes a sardonic interpretation of the dominant Victorian value of loyalty, particularly important in heroines.[23] Amelia's fifteen years of mourning and Dobbin's continuing courtship emerge as signs of aberration and delusion rather than heroism. They live in the past, clinging to dreams rather than confronting the reality of their lives. Love in each case rests on illusion and becomes but another aspect of the unreality inherent in Vanity Fair. Amelia deliberately suppresses her knowledge of George's unworthiness and transforms him into a false god: "All her husband's faults and foibles she had buried in the grave with him: she only remembered the lover, who had married her at all sacrifices; the noble husband so brave and beautiful, in whose arms she had hung on the morning when he had gone away to fight, and die gloriously for his king. From heaven the hero must be smiling down upon that paragon of a boy whom he had left to comfort and console her" (ch. 46). The bitter past turns into a comforting romance; husband and son become idols, their pictures her icons.

Dobbin participates in this theme of false worship and he, too, has an icon. He carries around with him a picture from a book of fashions, "fancying he saw some resemblance to Mrs. Osborne." Underlining the "fancying," the narrator adds: "perhaps, Mr. Dobbin's sentimental Amelia was no more like the real one than this absurd little print which he cherished" (ch. 43). But after fifteen years of being exploited by Amelia, Dobbin relinquishes the image and confronts her reality. "No, you are not worthy of the love which I have devoted to you," he tells her. "I knew all along that the prize I had set my life on was not worth the winning; that I was a fool, with fond fancies, too, bartering away my all of truth and ardour against your little feeble remnant of love. I will bargain no more: I withdraw" (ch. 66).

Dobbin's unexpected rebellion stimulates Amelia's regard and they marry. But it is too late. Once awakened, Dobbin can no longer love as he once did, and their reconciliation is muted and melancholy. As they embrace, the narrator stresses the disenchantment: "He has got the prize he has been trying for all his life. The bird has come in at last. . . . This is what he has asked for every day and hour for eighteen years. This is what he pined after. Here it is—the summit, the end—the last page of the third volume" (ch. 67). Characteristically, Thackeray provides the wished-for ending only to withhold its satisfactions.

Thackeray bids farewell to his romantic heroine in the famous valedictory image of the "tender little parasite." Although this is often read as a final puncturing of Amelia, it works rather as a summation of the complex presentation of her throughout the novel. The image fuses the two dominant narrative attitudes toward Amelia. On the one hand, there is the clear (and often bitter) exposure of the selfishness and ruthlessness involved in drawing life from another, as Amelia has always done; on the other, there is the indulgent tenderness which responds to her need. "I think it was her weakness which was her principal charm," the narrator comments at one point, "a kind of sweet submission and softness, which seemed to appeal to each man she met for his sympathy and protection" (ch. 38). As he well knows, weakness is as much a strategy of manipulation as Becky's more obvious artfulness, but Amelia's nature offers at least the recognition of human interdependence as Becky's does not. And in Vanity Fair this is, perhaps, a necessary illusion.

When Thackeray invokes Ecclesiastes in the concluding lines of the novel ("Ah! *Vanitas Vanitatum*! which of us is happy in this world?

Which of us has his desire? or, having it, is satisfied?"), he goes beyond social satire to uncover a radical flaw in the structure of life itself. This ending returns us to the beginning, to the prologue where the Manager of the Performance takes the reader around the bustling Fair, finding behind the scenes some humor and some kindness, "but the general impression is one more melancholy than mirthful. When you come home, you sit down in a sober, contemplative, not uncharitable frame of mind, and apply yourself to your books or your business" ("Before the Curtain"). This metaphor, he continues, is the only "moral" of his story. And the metaphor is a metaphor of reading. In Thackeray's vision of life fiction is an analogue for experience. To come home in a "contemplative, not uncharitable" frame of mind is to return to reality with heightened awareness and sympathy. It is to read correctly.

Chapter Four
The Thackerayan Hero:
The History of Pendennis

Like *Vanity Fair, The History of Pendennis* was illustrated by the author and first published in monthly parts, running from November 1848 to December 1850 with a three-month break (October–December 1849) when Thackeray was gravely ill and unable to write. Thackeray's gratitude to Dr. John Elliotson who treated him during this illness is conveyed in the dedication of *Pendennis* to Elliotson and in the sympathetic portrait of Dr. John Goodenough within the novel. The similarity between Goodenough's role in the life of Arthur Pendennis and that of Elliotson in the life of Thackeray underlines the autobiographical nature of *Pendennis.* As Gordon Ray has emphasized, Thackeray's novels all tend to draw heavily on real-life models, but *Pendennis* remains the closest to details of the author's own life.[1] While it should not be read as straight autobiography, its roots in Thackeray's personal history influence the tone and handling of the fiction.

"Our books are diaries," Thackeray wrote near the end of his life, "in which our feelings must of necessity be set down" ("De Finibus," *Roundabout Papers*). *Pendennis* resembles a diary in recording and reflecting on some of Thackeray's formative experiences and relationships. His own youth colors the youth of Arthur Pendennis whose home, Fairoaks in Clavering St. Mary, resembles Larkbeare in Ottery St. Mary where the young Thackeray spent several summers with his mother and stepfather. Thackeray's dissipation in university, his gambling, his halfhearted legal studies and entry into journalism are all reflected in Pen's career. Self-portraiture enters also into the characterization of George Warrington whose quasi-widowed state and impossible love for Laura Bell echo Thackeray's own peculiar marital situation and hopeless love for Jane Brookfield. But the emotional center of *Pendennis* is less Thackeray's love for Jane Brookfield (which is to animate his next novel, *The History of*

Henry Esmond) than his complex relationship with his mother which forms the basis for the remarkable portrait of Helen Pendennis. "Mrs. Pendennis is living with me (She is my mother)," Thackeray told a correspondent (*Letters*, 2:457).[2] Not only major characters like Helen and Arthur Pendennis but minor characters like Captain Shandon (based on William Maginn who edited *Fraser's Magazine* for which Thackeray wrote early in his career) come out of the author's life. In creating these characters Thackeray interprets and remembers, and this activity generates the meditative perspective of *Pendennis* where an older, tired narrator looks back with amusement, nostalgia, or regret at his own youth in telling the story of his naive and vain young hero.

Pendennis and the *Bildungsroman*

The strong autobiographical component in Thackeray's novel is characteristic of the *Bildungsroman*, the type of novel to which *Pendennis* belongs. The *Bildungsroman*, a novel about growing up, flourished through the nineteenth and into the twentieth century, reflecting in its subjective focus the modern interest in the self and its development. Typically, a *Bildungsroman* centers on a young boy (sometimes a young girl) who grows up in a secluded environment, feels restless, comes into conflict with a strong parental figure, and leaves home for a larger world where he plunges into the confusions of romantic love, the realities of society, and the problems of discovering one's proper vocation. All this turmoil works toward the achievement of adult identity, signaled most often by the correct choice of a mate and/or career. At the end of the novel the protagonist is poised, like Stephen Dedalus at the end of Joyce's *Portrait of the Artist*, on the threshold of maturity, having made the important initial decisions about the shape of his life. Variations of the pattern are numerous, especially when the protagonist is female, as in George Eliot's *The Mill on the Floss* which inverts much of the standard pattern. But all *Bildungsromane* have in common a focus on the formation of the self, on the movement of the protagonist from an uncertain to a more secure sense of identity.[3]

Pendennis establishes the pattern for all of Thackeray's later novels. From now on each novel is structured around the development of a protagonist from adolescence to maturity, detailing the trials along the way.[4] The trials of young Arthur Pendennis begin at the age of seventeen with his romantic confusion of sexual desire with love—a common enough error which Thackeray handles with a great deal of humor and compassionate insight, making the opening episode of *Pendennis* a classic evocation of the folly and vulnerability of adolescence. Pen himself is a healthy, bright, conceited youth accustomed to being worshipped by a doting mother, Helen Pendennis, and an equally doting foster-sister, Laura Bell, whom Helen inherited upon the death of Laura's father. Helen and Laura's father had fallen in love many years ago, but their love was frustrated by his foolish prior engagement to an older woman. So Helen settled for John Pendennis, more than twenty years older, who had also experienced frustration. Forced to leave university when his father died and to take up the demeaning trade of apothecary and surgeon, John Pendennis always longed to be a gentleman. Eventually, he succeeds in saving enough money to sell his shop and retire to a small country estate, Fairoaks, where his only son grows up convinced by the dubious family portraits in the dining room and by legends about the noble history of the Pendennises. The father is a minor figure in a family dominated by the mother-son relationship and dies when his son is sixteen. Pen exults secretly that his father's death makes him "the chief now and lord. He was Pendennis; and all round about him were servants and handmaids" (ch. 2). The "handmaids," presumably, include Laura and his mother.

Such a young man clearly has a lot to learn about the world and about himself, and his education begins with his sexual awakening. Sitting around writing gloomy Byronic verses, Pen feels the need of "a consuming passion." He rides out daily searching for his romantic ideal but finds her quite by chance when he bumps into an old school friend, Foker, who takes him to the theater. There Pen sees Emily Costigan, a twenty-six-year-old actress known professionally as Fotheringay, and he experiences "something overwhelming, maddening, delicious; a fever of wild joy and undefined longing" (ch. 4). Having learned love from reading romances, Pen is a naive lover and—like most Thackerayan lovers—he is deluded. In contrast to *Vanity Fair,* however, the delusion of Pen is a matter of comedy, and Thackeray creates rich humor out of the discrepancy between Pen's ideal Fotheringay and the good-natured but commonplace real woman.

Helen Pendennis does not find the situation amusing and summons Pen's uncle, the worldly old London bachelor, Major Pendennis, to straighten things out. Sacrificing his clubs and fashionable friends for the dullness of Fairoaks, Major Pendennis opens his campaign. Subtly, he works on Pen's snobbishness; less subtly, he informs Emily Costigan and her disreputable father than Pen has no money. "Sure, if he's no money, there's no use marrying him, Papa," Emily states matter-of-factly and goes on cleaning her shoes, pausing only briefly to regret "poor Arthur" (ch. 12).

Pen naturally falls into despair, writing poems and galloping wildly around the country, but he recovers quickly and begins to chafe at home, "eager to go forth again and try his restless wings" (ch. 16). He sets out for university, the second and more formal stage of Pen's education. Unlike the Fotheringay episode with its close focus and dramatic technique, the Oxbridge section consists mainly of indirect narration and so lacks the sharp, direct impact of the first episode. But it works effectively to create rapidly a more generalized impression of a longer experience: the three years at university. Rather like Thackeray himself, Pen begins college with academic aspirations which evaporate rapidly. After a term he drops mathematics in order to devote himself (he announces to his mother) to classical literature, only to discover that he in fact learns little from lectures and that private reading is really the most efficient form of study. With formal education out of the way, Pen concentrates on his social education, using the generous allowance provided by his fond mother to turn himself into a dandy complete with perfumed baths. He mixes with wealthier men, affects atheism, and learns to gamble. Predictably, Pen falls into debt, fails his final exams, and slinks out of Oxbridge. In a chapter entitled "Prodigal's Return" he comes home to his mother who welcomes him gratefully. At Laura's insistence (she has loaned him money for the debts) he goes back to take his degree and then returns to Fairoaks where he mopes around, bored and depressed but too poor to leave.

Life brightens when Sir Francis Clavering and his family move into the neighborhood, bringing with them the artificial Blanche Amory, Lady Clavering's daughter from an earlier marriage. Blanche and Pen exchange poems (he refurbishes some earlier verses) but both are only playing at love, although Helen Pendennis watches anxiously, fearing that her "darling project" of a Laura-Pen marriage is threatened. Helen pressures Pen into proposing to Laura: "Will you take me, dear Laura," he asks her, "and make our mother happy?" (ch. 27). To her credit Laura firmly refuses Pen's condescending proposal, and he is deeply relieved. After this interlude of experimentation with sexual relations, Pen embarks on the third major stage of his formation: experience in the city. He goes to London to study law but does little of that, especially after he moves in with the genial George Warrington who introduces Pen to the pleasures of drinking at the Back Kitchen and to the rough and lively world of journalism. A close-up view of the literary world leads to further disillusionment for Pen, but he adapts to it and earns money by writing critical articles, eventually producing a successful autobiographical novel in the fashionable mode.[5]

Pen is now twenty-five years old, a jaded man of the world who regards his youthful passion as "the period of my little illusions" and decides to marry Blanche Amory for money. In this mood he meets Fanny Bolton, a working-class girl who sees Pen as a hero out of a novel. He in turn patronizes her and finds her attractive but resists the temptation of seduction out of a sense of honor. At Fairoaks, however, Helen Pendennis has heard that Pen and Fanny are lovers and hates the woman whom she sees as responsible for her son's "fall." When Pen falls seriously ill (largely as a result of frustrated desire), Helen rushes up to London and finds Fanny nursing him. Ruthlessly, she shuts Fanny out. Nor is Laura, with whom the married but separated Warrington now falls in love, any more compassionate. Upon Pen's recovery he is no longer tormented by desire for Fanny, but she continues to be a cause of estrangement between mother and son. The tension explodes finally and matters are sorted out just before Helen dies, reconciled to her son.

With Helen's death the novel loses a pivotal character and suffers as a result. The loss of his mother signals the symbolic end of Pen's childhood, but Thackeray tends to drag out the question of what sort of adult he will become. It takes almost two hundred pages to rescue Pen from the cynicism into which he has drifted. Helen dies in Chapter 57; Pen reencounters Laura in Chapter 66; they marry in Chapter 75. The novel's final section relies heavily for its action on a complicated subplot involving Blanche's father, Amory (known as Altamont), supposedly dead but actually alive and blackmailing Sir Francis Clavering. Major Pendennis (who has recognized Amory) does some blackmailing himself to obtain from Sir Francis generous terms for Pen upon marrying Blanche. When Pen discovers his uncle's activities and Blanche's real identity (she is an illegitimate, convict's daughter), he resolves reluctantly to do the honorable thing: refuse the generous terms and marry Blanche anyway. By this time Pen is in love with Laura who supports his decision. Fortunately, Blanche has been toying with Pen's old friend, Foker, and he discovers them together in a scene reminiscent of Rawdon's discovery of Becky and Lord Steyne in *Vanity Fair*. The way is now clear for Laura and Pen who marry and settle at Fairoaks where Pen writes and serves as Member of Parliament for the district.

Arthur Pendennis and Victorian Skepticism

Although Thackeray is not an intellectual writer (his contemporary, W. C. Roscoe, declared that there is "a total absence in his books of what we usually call ideas"),[6] he does reflect the intellectual currents of his age. Most particularly, as Roscoe himself stressed, Thackeray participates in its uncertainty and skepticism: "We apprehend he never asked 'why?' in his life, except perhaps to prove to another that he had no because."[7] More than his other novels, *Pendennis* expresses and examines this state of mind, linking it to its historical context. Almost twenty years before *Pendennis,* Thackeray's old target, Edward Bulwer-Lytton, wrote that "we live in an age of visible transition—an age of disquietude and doubt," a definition of the age that was to be reformulated constantly for the rest of the century.[8] As Bulwer's comment suggests, the Victorian world was profoundly insecure and self-conscious, acutely aware of the loss of certainty and traditional authority, especially in religion. During the last year of the serialization of *Pendennis,* Tennyson published his great confrontation with doubt, *In Memoriam* (1850), and in the following year Thomas Carlyle declared: "No fixed highways more; the old spiritual highways and recognized paths to the Eternal, now all torn-up and flung in heaps. . . ."[9] Matthew Arnold, the Victorian poet closest to Thackeray in many respects, analyzed obsessively what he called "this strange disease of modern life," summing up in the famous lines of "Stanzas from the Grande Chartreuse" the Victorian sense of alienation in the world: "Wandering between two worlds, one dead, / The other powerless to be born / With nowhere yet to rest my head."[10]

Pendennis comes out of the 1840's, a particularly turbulent decade that increased the sense of insecurity and bewilderment. "The Hungry 40s" were marked in England by the beginning of free trade; by the rise of industrial protest as workers organized the Chartist movement, a demand for a more democratic system; by the "railway mania" which in a few years changed the face of the landscape and the speed of life; by the demoralization of the established Anglican church as bright young men converted to Rome under the influence of the famous 1845 conversion of John Henry Newman.[11] Ireland suffered its near-fatal potato famine in 1846, while in 1848 (the year of Marx and Engels, *The Communist Manifesto*) Europe erupted into a series of revolutions that shook the foundations of traditional order. Thackeray, who was not very interested in politics, nevertheless recognized the spirit of the time, telling his mother in July 1848 that "there is an awful time coming for all of us" (*Letters*, 2:409). A few years later he cheerfully reiterated that "the great revolution's a coming" and added: "The present writers are all employed as by instinct in unscrewing the old framework of society, and get it ready for the Smash. I take a sort of pleasure in my little part in the business and in saying destructive things in a good humoured jolly way" (*Letters*, 2:761). Clearly, Thackeray did not regard "the Smash" very seriously, but, equally clearly, he relished participating in the new, challenging energies generated by early Victorian society as it set about "unscrewing the old framework of society."

This cultural context informs the function of Arthur Pendennis and the shape of his life. In Pen, Thackeray deliberately creates a representative nineteenth-century man, a figure who (in the final words of the novel) "does not claim to be a hero, but only a man and a brother." Pen himself is acutely aware that he is marked by his particular historical moment and defines "our era and period of civilization" as one of accelerated growth and change. "Ye gods!" he exclaims to Warrington, "how rapidly we live and grow!" (ch.44). Through Pen's story Thackeray articulates his sense of experiences and problems typical of his age, for the novel is not just about growing up but about growing up Victorian. And like his major contemporaries Thackeray saw as the central problem of his time the difficulty of finding adequate sources of value and belief: Pen is representative largely because he lacks certainty.

Once he has left his secure, country home and rejected the traditional values represented by Helen (and Laura), Pen is adrift, trying one value system after another and allowing time and circumstances to form his identity. To remain in the country with Helen and her genteel circle is to withdraw from the mainstream of modern urban society. Significantly, the congregation of Helen's Anglican church is not only dwindling but is devoid of appeal for the factory workers who have recently moved into the area. Pen is eager to join the mainstream, but he is curiously passive and becomes increasingly so as he grows older, as if his surrender to his age has drained him of energy and initiative. Phrases like "fickle," "easily led," "easily adapting himself to all whom he met" emphasize Pen's passivity, fluctuations, and adaptability. In a few years the ardent young lover of Emily Costigan has turned into the listless pursuer of Blanche Amory. Lacking any consistent inner principles, having no firm purpose, Pen is particularly vulnerable to disillusionment and to a sense of the futility of life. Thackeray's contemporaries recognized in the character of Pen a sign of the times. "The irresolute, half-ashamed, sceptical hero," wrote Fitzjames Stephen of Pen in 1855, ". . . governed by tastes and circumstances instead of principles . . . not very bad, nor very good, nor very anything . . . is one of the saddest, as it is one of the most masterly memorials of the times in which he lived which any writer ever drew for posterity."[12]

The relationship between Pen's skepticism and nineteenth-century experience is drawn most explicitly in Chapter 61, "The Way of the World," where Pen argues with Warrington about problems of principle and truth and where "the reader may perhaps see allusions to questions which, no doubt, have occupied and discomposed himself." Invoking nineteenth-century politicians and events, Pen claims that observation of contemporary politics demonstrates the futility of ideals and of individual action against the force of "circumstances." The contrast between the promises of Whigs in an election and their actions when in power, for example, proves only that "they submit to circumstances which are stronger than they." Pen's own language is full of constructions like "I wait," "I submit," "I acquiesce" because he can find no certain values to provide him with a basis for action and judgment. The root of his difficulty is uncertainty about truth. Human judgment, he tells Warrington, is inherently limited: "We admire this man as being a great philosopher, and set down the other as a dullard, not knowing either, or the amount of truth in either or being certain of the truth anywhere."

In a reference to the religious controversies of the 1840s Pen explicitly connects this skepticism with the historical moment in which he lives. "Where is the truth?" he asks and replies that he sees it "on both sides" in questions of politics and religion, isolating for emphasis the case of the Newman brothers: John Henry Newman, the celebrated Anglican who converted to Roman Catholicism and wrote a fictional account of his experience in *Loss and Gain* (1848), and Francis Newman, the classics professor who rejected the Christian church and published an account of his religious thought in *Phases of Faith* (1850). "I see the truth in that man," Pen says of John Henry Newman, "as I do in his brother, whose logic drives him to quite a different conclusion, and who, after having passed a life in vain endeavours to reconcile an irreconcilable book, flings it at last down in despair, and declares, with tearful eyes, and hands up to Heaven, his revolt and recantation. If the truth is with all these, why should I take side with any one of them?" (ch.61). Two individuals, equally sincere, have perceived a different truth, and this challenges the idea of an absolute or certain truth available to all in the same way.

Over a hundred years earlier Alexander Pope could confidently advise readers to turn to "Unerring Nature, Still divinely bright, / One clear, unchang'd, and Universal Light."[13] But by the time of *Pendennis* the light was less clear and a modern sense of the subjectivity of reality had begun to take over, as we see early in the novel when the narrator sighs: "Ah! sir—a distinct universe walks about under your hat and under mine—all things in nature are different to each" (ch. 16). In Chapter 61 Pen illustrates how contemporary history could fragment the notion of truth and engender this unsettling conviction that "all things in nature are different to each." While Thackeray does not endorse Pen's skepticism, pointing out its elements of facile and self-interested reasoning, he does maintain that Pen is not a "truth-avoiding" man. For all his faults and failures, Pen represents the dilemma of his culture, cut off from traditional sources of value and unable to find adequate replacements.

Pendennis as Moral Fable

At once a comic *Bildungsroman* and a serious definition of the Victorian sensibility, *Pendennis* also functions as a moral fable. "Our profession seems to me to be as serious as the Parson's own," Thackeray wrote at the time of *Vanity Fair* (*Letters,* 2:282). A concept of the novelist as secular preacher or, in Thackeray's own phrase, as "week-day preacher" ("Swift," *The English Humourists*) informs *Pendennis,* beginning with its structure which is shaped by the parable of the Prodigal Son. The novel's overall pattern of defiance of traditional authority, disillusioning experience in the larger world, and remorseful return to home and parent (or surrogate parent in this case) recalls the biblical story. And Thackeray ensures that we make the connection by including several explicit references to the parable within the text (e.g., chs. 21, 28). The illustration that Thackeray drew for the title page of *Pendennis* alerts us to the specific moral theme on which the novel is to focus. The drawing shows Arthur Pendennis standing between two female figures. On one side a half-naked blond mermaid clings to him; on the other he is caught in the embrace of a dark-haired domestic figure in Victorian dress. Behind this domestic figure rises a church (in half ruin), at her feet stands a cherub; behind the mermaid stretches the sea and at her feet lurks a devil. Pen gazes at the blond siren but he has already begun to move toward the domestic heroine.[14]

This drawing points to the theme of moral choice, establishing Blanche Amory and Laura Bell as signs of the alternatives available to Pen. What is

Title page of the first bound edition of *Pendennis*

at stake is the question of how Pen is to live his life, whether by worldly or unworldly values, for he must decide between what the novel calls "the sentimental life" and "the practical life." Each heroine is supported in turn by an authority figure from the older generation, so that Pen's decision involves a further choice between Major Pendennis, who busies himself setting up the engagement with Blanche, and Helen Pendennis, whose spirit hovers over the romance of Laura and Pen. Through the opposition between the two heroines and the two parental figures Thackeray examines the meaning and consequences of living by worldly values (like social or financial success) and living by unworldly values (like love and loyalty). The novel is filled with contrasts, tensions, and parallels which reinforce and deepen the illustration of the theme on the title page. Distinctions between country and city, art and life, clubs and church help to establish the conflicting values, while the various lovers from Foker to the musician Bows to the curate Smirke generate ironic resonances which reflect on Pen in his different stages. His cynicism about Blanche, for example, is underscored vividly when Thackeray shows Pen throwing his rose from Blanche in the gutter, while Foker carefully places his rose from her in a glass of water (ch.45).

In *Pendennis* Thackeray continues his exploration of Vanity Fair and focuses in particular on the artifice of a worldly existence. The note is struck immediately in the opening paragraph of the novel which introduces Major Pendennis in his club and provides a detailed description of his clothes. "At a distance, or seeing his back merely," the narrator comments, "you would have taken him to be not more than thirty years old: it was only by a nearer inspection that you saw the factitious nature of his rich brown hair." Pen's "selfish old Mentor" has his moments of real feeling, but Major Pendennis has devoted his life to the creation of a role and cannot exist without it. He typifies the world of *Pendennis* where role playing is pervasive and the distinction between the person and the role is often obscure.[15] Pen begins by confusing the two in Emily Costigan, and it is entirely appropriate that his first step into the adult world take the form of his falling in love with an actress whose mechanical stage gestures he interprets as signifying authentic emotions. Pen himself soon learns to play roles, acting the romantic lover with Blanche Amory, the novel's consummate actress who continually turns life into a "pretty little drama."

Blanche epitomizes artifice. Her name itself is false, having been changed from Betsy; her language is sprinkled pretentiously with French phrases; her very blondness is fake. The most calculated of creatures, she affects spontaneity; unable to feel, she projects an image of herself as a person of unusual sensibility and imitates emotions in verse. "Oh, Major Pendennis, I am sick of London, and of balls, and of young dandies," she sighs at one point, proclaiming her desire to enter a convent because she is alone and misunderstood: "I wish to quit the world. I am not very old: but I am tired, I have suffered so much—I've been so disillusionated—I'm weary, I'm weary—oh! that the Angel of Death would come and beckon me away!" The narrator immediately punctures her posing: "This speech may be interpreted as follows. A few nights since a great lady, Lady Flamingo, had cut Miss Amory and Lady Clavering. She was quite mad because she could not get an invitation to Lady Drum's ball: it was the end of the season and nobody had proposed to her; she had made no sensation at all" (ch.44).

Image patterns also serve to define Blanche. Where Laura is often seen out of doors and is linked to freshness and nature, Blanche is shown mainly indoors and associated with imitations and perversions of nature. Shortly after her introduction, for instance, Mirobolant (the French chef who wants to marry an *"Anglaise"* and has chosen Blanche) describes the elegant dinner he created for her in tribute to her name and habit of dressing in white. "I determined that my dinner should be as spotless as the snow," he begins and details how he made a white soup (*potage à la Reine Blanche*), fashioned sweetbread and chicken and assorted other pale dishes, "and the only brown thing which I permitted myself in the entertainment was a little roast of lamb, which I laid in a meadow of spinaches, surrounded by croustillons, representing sheep, and or- namented with daisies and other savage flowers" (ch.23). It is all very clever and rather repellent. The evocation of sheep, meadows, and flowers only underlines how far the whole scene is from the real thing. Cunning imitation characterizes both Blanche and the dinner fabricated for her. Laura, in contrast, is caught a few pages later "as she came in from the garden . . . her cheeks rather flushed, her looks frank and smiling—a basket of roses in her hand" (ch.24).

Blanche exists in what John Loofbourow has called the "insipid artifice" of degraded pastoral.[16] Deriving from classical Greek poetry, pastoral is marked by the artful imitation of the simplicity and innocence that urban dwellers often imagine to be typical of the country. At its most persuasive, pastoral can express the timeless human dream of a green world of youth and innocence (as in some of Shakespeare's romantic comedies), but it can also degenerate into mere affectation, triviality, and sentimentality, as in the well-known story of Queen Marie Antoinette of France playing at being a shepherdess. So Blanche plays at being an artless "Sylph" and inhabits a London drawing room whose overblown pastoral motifs represent the degradation of the original dream into third-rate interior decoration. On the fluffy white carpets "bloomed roses and tulips as big as warming-pans" and everywhere "there were Dresden shepherds and shepherdesses convenient at your elbow; there were, moreover, light-blue poodles and ducks and cocks and hens in porcelain" (ch.37). Blanche moves easily amid such artificial figures, for she is herself swallowed up by the artifice she has created. Blanche becomes "a monstrous figure . . . because she becomes incapable of distinguishing between performance and reality."[17] Here Blanche differs decisively from Becky Sharp in *Vanity Fair* who knows well the difference. But for Blanche the only reality is in performance. This is why she is so threatened when Pen refuses to play her romantic game toward the end of the novel. "Why ask me to feign raptures and counterfeit romance, in which neither of us believe?" he says, and Blanche responds with "a queer piteous look" (ch.64). "Sham" is the only reality she knows. Not surprisingly, she destroys her chance of marriage with Foker, who genuinely loves her, and marries a dubious Parisian count.

The Problem of Time

When Pen chooses Laura over Blanche, he saves himself from turning either into the kind of soulless, restless creature represented by Blanche or into the more sympathetic but still radically flawed model of worldliness represented by Major Pendennis. Most important, he saves himself from simply drifting on the current of time, one moment following the other with nothing to link them into significance. The problem of time—how to cope with its relentless movement, how to give meaning to its inevitable erosion of life—comes into prominence in *Pendennis* and is to remain a central problem in Thackeray's novels.[18] Major Pendennis is a memorable figure, something more than a comic or satiric character, largely because he is growing old: "He began to own that he was no longer of the present age, and dimly to apprehend that the young men laughed at him" (ch.67). For a "man of fashion" whose whole being is invested in being in fashion, such a recognition is devastating. But the sense of isolation that grows on Major Pendennis is not confined to worldly old gentlemen. Permeating the entire novel is a view of isolation as an inescapable condition of human existence. "You and I are but a pair of infinite isolations, with some fellow-islands a little more or less near to us," the narrator tells the reader (ch. 16). The death that time brings to all of us only heightens the isolation. When the narrator imagines two contrasting ends to the "voyage of life" in Chapter 59, he sees one hypothetical individual as successful in life and the other as drowning in the ocean. But both are ultimately alone—"alone on the hopeless spar, drowning out of sight; alone in the midst of the crowd applauding you."

Women like Helen and Laura can ease the burden of existence and give life a larger meaning. Such women are the familiar saving angels of Victorian fiction.[19] Sheltered from the corrupting world, they remain in touch with timeless spiritual values and are able to rescue the male protagonist from an empty or vicious life. "Teach me my duty," Pen begs Laura. "Pray for me that I may do it—pure heart" (ch. 70). Laura is an extension of Helen, a living surrogate for the dead mother. When Pen meets Laura again months after Helen's death, he sees Laura as "his mother's legacy to him," while Laura's first words to Pen are, "Mamma left you to me" (ch. 66). Her function is especially clear in the scene recounting her acceptance of Pen: "Pendennis's head sinks down in the girl's lap, as he sobs out, 'Come and bless us, dear mother,' and arms as tender as Helen's once more enfold him" (ch. 74). This embrace in which mother and wife merge links Pen's past, present, and future, giving his life a coherent shape. Time is no longer mere succession but a comforting circle presided over by a personal deity. Helen's will has been done.

"Victorian fiction," J. Hillis Miller has noted, "may be said to have as its fundamental theme an exploration of the various ways in which a man may seek to make a god of another person in a world without God."[20] In Thackeray's world this deification—and meaning generally—depend on the power of memory. Remembrance of the past creates and supports the image of Helen which sustains Pen at the end of the novel. Scattered throughout the novel are moments when Pen remembers, as in the following passage where he recalls the time when he and Helen read together the popular book of devotional poetry, John Keble's *The Christian Year* (1827): "The son and mother whispered it to each other with awe—Faint, very faint, and seldom in after-life Pendennis heard that solemn church-music: but he always loved the remembrance of it, and of the times when it struck on his heart, and he walked over the fields full of hope and void of doubt, as the church-bells rang on Sunday morning" (ch. 3). Pen typically remembers moments like this which evoke a past of emotional and psychological security rooted in Helen and in the religious certainty associated with her. When Pen revisits Fairoaks late in the novel, he recalls the summer evenings of childhood when he was "sheltered as yet from the world's contamination in the pure and anxious bosom of love" (ch.65).

Nostalgia for the security and faith of childhood was characteristic of skeptical Victorians to whom "home became the place where one *had* been at peace and childhood a blessed time when truth was certain and doubt with its divisive effects unknown."[21] But in *Pendennis* nostalgia becomes faith (Helen is a "saint") because sanctioning Pen's memories are the displaced emotions of religious belief. At several key points in the novel Pen prays, and thoughts of God are usually entangled with thoughts of mother. It is Helen who stimulates the traditional religious feelings, but she does not do so directly. These emotions are released only through memory, for to Pen faith can be recaptured only through the mediation of memory. This is quite apparent in the prayer scene that directly precedes Helen's death. Mother and son have reconciled, a reconciliation brought about at least partially by the recognition that soon they will be separated permanently. "As they were talking the clock struck nine," we are told, "and Helen reminded him how, when he was a little boy, she used to go up to his bedroom at that hour, and hear him say Our Father. And once more, oh, once more, the young man fell down at his mother's sacred knees, and sobbed out the prayer" (ch.57). Such moments, drawing on basic religious emotions, generate the myth of Helen after her death when, Robert Bledsoe suggests, she becomes more powerful than in life "since now Helen is not just a presence, but a Presence."[22]

As Pen's memory slowly fashions this sustaining Presence, the novel simultaneously exposes the complicated woman whose "maternal infatuation" oppresses even as it soothes her son. Although Pen's memories are woven out of actual experiences, they are partial and partially self-deceptive. For much of the narrative Pen has struggled to free himself from home and mother, and his one moment of aggression is directed against Helen. In the powerful explosion of domestic tensions that directly precedes Helen's death, Pen turns on his mother for having intercepted a letter from Fanny Bolton. Significantly, Laura repeatedly begs Pen to contain his anger lest he "kill" the ailing Helen, and Pen's persistence in attacking his mother suggests a deeply rooted hostility. Helen's worship of her son has resulted in a blind and strangling possessiveness damaging in its results on Pen's character and on her own, breeding in Helen a cruel heedlessness of the emotions of others. Her devotion to Pen has made her unjust to Laura, to Warrington, and—most damningly—to Fanny Bolton whom she regards with a face "hopelessly cruel and ruthless" and whom she abruptly and callously turns out. Helen's behavior to everyone in this episode of Pen's illness, in fact, underlines the obsessive nature of her maternal love. "She had closed the door upon Major Pendennis, and Laura, too; and taken possession of her son" (ch.52).

This problematic Helen is excluded from the memories that form the basis of the private myth Pen accepts at the end of the novel. But the myth does allow him to regain his capacity for feeling and his integrity, and Thackeray avoids simplistic conclusions by noting that Pen's skepticism remains active. A few chapters before the conclusion, when Pendennis is already in love with Laura, the two have a conversation in which Pendennis tells her, "I think for some of you there has been no fall." But Laura detects "a sneer coming," and Pendennis replies:

"A sneer, is there? I was thinking, my dear, that nature in making you so good and loving did very well: but—"

"But what? What is the wicked but? and why are you always calling it up?"

"But will come in spite of us. But is reflection. But is the sceptic's familiar, with whom he has made a compact; and if he forgets it, and indulges in happy day-dreams, or building of air-castles, or listens to sweet music, let us say, or to the bells ringing to church, But taps at the door, and says, Master, I am here. You are my master; but I am yours. Go where you will you can't travel without me. I will whisper to you when you are on your knees at church. I will be at your marriage pillow. I will sit down at your table with your children. I will be behind your death-bed curtain. That is what But is," Pen said. (ch. 71).

Pen sees "But" attacking the affirmative activity of the imagination and the basic value-making institutions of his time: religion and family. At the moment of death "But" creeps up to whisper that death is indeed all. Saving angels, it seems, may rescue a man from the dangerous sirens of the world, but they are finally powerless to still the restless movement of the skeptical mind. Pen knows that his assent to Helen and Laura can be only provisional: his "But" will always be there.

Chapter Five

The Uses of History:
The History of Henry Esmond

Writing and Reception

"I've got a better subject for a novel than any I've yet had," Thackeray declared when he finished *Pendennis* in November 1850 (*Letters*, 2:708), and this subject he embodied almost two years later in the three volumes of *The History of Henry Esmond, Esq. A Colonel in the Service of her Majesty Q. Anne: Written by Himself* (1852).[1] *Henry Esmond* was a departure for Thackeray, whose reputation was built on satiric analysis of contemporary society, and George Henry Lewes warned readers expecting a "comic novel" that the new work was "as unlike *Vanity Fair* and *Pendennis* as a book written by Thackeray can be."[2] Abandoning the familiar world of his earlier successes for the more remote eighteenth century of Augustan England, Thackeray also exchanged the informal voice characteristic of his third-person narrator for the formal cadences of Henry Esmond's first-person narration. Thackeray's unusual seriousness about *Henry Esmond* is reflected in its unique status in his canon: it is the only novel to be written completely before publication. "Its much too grave & sad for [serial publication]," he told his mother, "& the incident not sufficient" (*Letters*, 3:24). Recognizing the interdependence of form and content, Thackeray sought a more congenial method of publication that would allow him to establish the rhythms and maintain the moods appropriate to the more inward concerns of his new novel.

Thackeray's rejection of part publication also involved an effort at literal realism. Anxious to sustain the illusion of the eighteenth century which he had worked to create within the fiction by his diction, allusions, and style, Thackeray wanted to ensure that the novel's outward form would be consistent with his attempt at historical reconstruction. Accordingly, *Henry Esmond* was published in the type face and in the three-volume format typical of the eighteenth century. Such fidelity was reinforced by the inclusion of old-fashioned spelling and of period conventions like the dedication and form of the title. In its original edition the book was a skillful imitation of memoirs of the previous century.

That century had long interested Thackeray—his first important fictions, *Catherine* and *Barry Lyndon,* both take place in the 1700s—but at the time of *Henry Esmond* his interest was particularly intense. In the summer of 1851, shortly before he began the novel, Thackeray delivered his successful lecture series, *The English Humourists of the Eighteenth Century.* To prepare himself for these lectures, he had steeped himself in the writing of the period. The intimacy he gained from researching and repeating the lectures (Thackeray toured his humorists over England, Scotland, and the United States) developed his ease with the language and style of the time and made him familiar with the background of *Henry Esmond.* The facility with which the novel captures the atmosphere of the age of Queen Anne was a constant theme in Victorian reviews, even the unsympathetic John Forster observing that Thackeray's style betrayed "no excess, no strain after effect."[3] There was less agreement, however, on the wisdom of Thackeray's decision to enter into and imitate a past age, some readers feeling that he had unnecessarily restricted his talents and devoted his energies to a rather hollow enterprise. The influential *Times* review set the tone here in its direct address to the author: "Why, Mr. Thackeray, in the name of all that is rational, why write in fetters?"[4]

Thackeray, of course, never claimed that writing novels was a particularly rational process. And at the time of *Henry Esmond* he was in a less rational state of mind than usual. In September 1851 under pressure from her husband Jane Brookfield broke with Thackeray, leaving him devastated and volatile, his moods swinging from passionate devotion to intense bitterness. "I wish that I had never loved her," he stated at the time and threw himself into his novel (*Letters,* 4:431). The concentration the book demanded ("[*Henry Esmond*] occupies me to the exclusion of the 19th century pretty well") provided a needed refuge, distraction and distance from the emotional turmoil of his present, a period he later summed up as "a period of grief and pain so severe that I dont like to think of it" (*Letters,* 3:24). This period, Gordon Ray has shown, shapes *Henry Esmond,* a work dominated by Thackeray's experience of love and loss.[5] The novel refracts and rewrites his relationship with Jane Brookfield, offering both an acute psychological analysis of love and a wish-fulfilling dream. Thackeray himself was always frank about the link between this novel and his own condition, reporting that "I am writing a book of cutthroat melancholy suitable to my state" (*Letters*, 2:807) and identifying Esmond to his mother as "a handsome likeness of an ugly son of yours" (*Letters*, 2:815). George Henry Lewes was one contemporary reader who responded to the novel's emotional authenticity. "All who have *lived*," he asserted, "will have felt the pulse of real suffering . . . here."[6]

Not all readers were quite so sympathetic, the complicated relationship between Rachel and Esmond (with its incestuous undertones) proving troublesome even to progressive minds like that of George Eliot. In an often-quoted remark Eliot declared *Henry Esmond* "the most uncomfortable book you can imagine. . . . The hero is in love with the daughter all through the book and marries the mother at the end."[7] Echoing her discomfort, the *Athenaeum* was more explicit, seeing Esmond's marriage as "like a marriage with his own mother," while the popular novelist, Margaret Oliphant, stated flatly that "our most sacred sentiments are outraged."[8] Such reaction suggests why reviewers concentrated on the novel's artistry rather than on its themes and may account for the disappointing sales of *Henry Esmond*. "Here is the *very* best I can do," Thackeray announced when it was published.[9] But in later years he felt that he had failed ("Nobody reads it") and dismissed his own hero, telling Anthony Trollope: "After all, Esmond was a prig."[10]

The Theme of Identity

Henry Esmond follows the *Bildungsroman* pattern of *Pendennis* in telling the story of the maturation of a young man. Like the earlier novel it defines the problems of choice and values central to the formation of the adult self through the hero's response to two women: one a vain and worldly creature, one a loving and faithful domestic heroine. But in *Henry Esmond* the focus is more internal, the exploration more subjective, for Esmond tells his own story. An old man in America around 1740, he looks back at the decisive years in England from 1690 to 1714 when he became who he is.[11] In eighteenth-century style Esmond usually talks of himself in the third person, modulating occasionally to "I" or "we," a habit creating the sense of distance and of shifting intensity which gives the work its air of being an ongoing meditation about both his own life and human life in general.

Significantly, Esmond chooses to begin with a particular moment in 1691 when he was twelve years old. A lonely boy, he sits reading one day in the portrait gallery of Castlewood when he looks up to find a dazzling, golden-haired woman stretching out her hand to him. This beatific vision proves to be twenty-year-old Rachel Esmond, the Viscountess Castlewood, who has come to take possession of Castlewood with her husband, Francis the fourth Viscount, and her two children, Beatrix and Frank. After re-creating this moment, Esmond circles back, accounting for the years leading up to it and concentrating on his life after his sudden removal from an uncongenial foster home by the chaplain of the third Viscount Castlewood. The chaplain, Father Holt, tells the boy who knows himself as Henry Thomas that henceforth he will be called Harry Esmond (Esmond being the family name of the Viscounts Castlewood). Young Harry learns eventually that he is reputedly the illegitimate son of the current Viscount, Thomas, whose household he now joins as page to the imperious Lady Castlewood. But the central figure in his life at this time is the Jesuit priest, Holt, who inspires him with affection and religious zeal and whose secret activities add excitement to the boy's existence.

After the 1688 fall of the Catholic Stuart king James II and the installation of the Protestant William of Orange as monarch, Holt's mysterious behavior increases, for he and Lord Castlewood plot the restoration of James Stuart. One of their failed plots brings soldiers to Castlewood who come to arrest the Viscount. Finding that he has fled to Ireland, they arrest his wife instead and Esmond is left behind, "belonging as it were to nobody, and quite alone in the world" (bk. 1, ch. 6). When his father dies (wounded in a battle against William of Orange), Esmond awaits the new Lord Castlewood "with no small anxiety." That anxiety is relieved by his meeting with the new family, more particularly by his meeting with the warm, maternal Rachel described in the opening scene of his memoirs. After their arrival, Esmond exchanges Holt's Catholicism for Rachel's Anglicanism and enters upon "the happiest period of all his life" (bk. 1, ch. 7).

The idyll is shattered when, at the age of sixteen, he visits the "bouncing" daughter of the village blacksmith and brings home smallpox. Rachel turns on him in fury, demanding that he "pollute the place no more" (bk. 1, ch. 8). Her anger (prompted in part by a sexual jealousy she does not recognize) abates quickly; but after she and Esmond recover from smallpox, Rachel encourages him to go to Cambridge where he has an undistinguished career. She herself, meanwhile, endures an increasingly strained marriage, and Esmond comes to recognize sadly that "the persons whom he loved best in the world . . . were living unhappily together" (bk. 1, ch. 11). Matters come to a crisis when Lord Castlewood becomes jealous of the dashing rake, Lord Mohun, and provokes a duel in which Esmond participates. Mortally wounded in the duel, Castlewood dictates a dying confession revealing that Esmond is indeed legitimate and the lawful Viscount Castlewood. Book 1 ends with Esmond, now aware of his true identity, burning the confession dispossessing Rachel and her children and giving himself up to prison authorities for his part in the illegal duel.

Book 2 opens with the widowed Rachel's visit to Esmond in prison, a scene which recalls but reverses the striking opening scene of the novel where Rachel had stretched out her hand in acceptance. Now she refuses her hand and bursts into hysterical denunciation, accusing Esmond of allowing her husband to be murdered. He suffers silently her unjust reproaches, then violently strikes his own wounded hand against the wall and falls unconscious. Recovery leaves him depressed and bitter: "And this was the return for a life of devotion" (bk. 2, ch. 1). Released from prison and restless, Esmond joins the army where, despite introduction to the brutalities and stupidities of war, he recovers his spirits. A year later he seeks out Rachel who this time extends her hand and begs his forgiveness. Her half-conscious passion for Esmond now becomes more apparent, and he proposes that she come with him to the family estate in Virginia to begin "a new life in a new world" (bk. 2, ch. 6). Rachel refuses, and Esmond soon forgets his impulsive offer under the impact of seeing her daughter, Beatrix, again. In the celebrated scene of Beatrix descending the stairs Esmond becomes enchanted by her lustrous beauty, spending the next several years (and the rest of Book 2) striving for promotion and military distinction in an effort to win this woman whom he knows full well to be unobtainable and a vain coquette. Beatrix tolerates Esmond but her sparkle is reserved for more splendid possibilities. While on the Continent with the army, Esmond reencounters Father Holt (as devoted to mysteries as ever) who tells him his mother's history and directs him to her grave.

Having established Esmond's past, the novel moves in Book 3 toward resolving his future by working out the problem of Beatrix to whom he remains "enthralled." He leaves the army and dabbles in literature, writing a transparently autobiographical comedy entitled, "The Faithful Fool." The audience yawns. But Rachel is more patient, serving Esmond (whose secret she has learned) as a faithful confidante of his feelings for her daughter. At the age of twenty-six Beatrix, having been repeatedly engaged and disengaged, prepares seriously to marry the wealthy, elderly Duke of Hamilton. Shortly before the wedding, however, he dies in a duel with the same Mohun who had killed Lord Castlewood. Esmond's hopes revive. In a last effort to win Beatrix, a firm supporter of the exiled Stuarts, he engages in a plot to place on the throne upon the death of Queen Anne the Stuart claimant, James Edward.

This "momentous game" for the throne of England is played and almost won, but at the crucial moment James Edward is dallying with Beatrix at Castlewood instead of leading his followers in London. Disillusioned, Esmond repudiates the Stuarts, breaking his sword in front of the Stuart prince, and he resigns absolutely all claims to the Castlewood title by burning the recently discovered documentary evidence of his right. Beatrix is also swept away in this general rejection of past allegiances, for Esmond discovers that "his love of ten years was over" (bk. 3, ch. 13). Exchanging the Old World for the New as he had once proposed, Esmond marries Rachel and settles in the new Castlewood in Virginia where he grows into a serene old age and writes his memoirs for his grandsons.

Esmond's choice of audience illustrates his lifelong concern with his familial identity. Himself unaware for years whose son he was, his very name changing mysteriously from Henry Thomas to Henry Esmond, he now ensures that his own male heirs will know their name and their origins. In telling his story, Esmond records his childhood insecurity and anxiety about his obscure birth. "Who was he and what?" he wonders the night he learns that his father is dead. "Why here rather than elsewhere?" (bk. 1, ch. 6). Thinking himself a bastard, he sees himself as an outcast and thinks "with many a pang of shame and grief of his strange and solitary condition:—how he had a father and no father; a nameless mother that had been brought to ruin, perhaps, by that very father whom Harry could only acknowledge in secret and with a blush" (bk. 1, ch. 6). Such feelings shape Esmond's adult psyche which remains obsessed with mothers and fathers. As J. Hillis Miller points out, the novel is "a chain of overlapping patterns . . . each reconstituting the universal family relationships: mother, mistress, sister, father, brother, son."[12] Starved for family, Esmond typically sees those around him only in these roles, and his own role as son and pseudo-son is of paramount importance to him. Long before Freud defined the Oedipus complex, Thackeray has his obsessed son sign himself "Oedipus" (bk. 3, ch. 3), and Esmond fulfills the classic oedipal fantasy of supplanting the father figure (significantly, Castlewood is killed by a man with the same first name as Esmond) and marrying the mother. But the fantasy also operates more subtly, informing as well Esmond's renunciation of the title where he acts out the role of the good father surrendering generously the authority that is rightfully his to Rachel's son, Frank, and so countering the behavior of his own bad father who had dispossessed his son. Esmond early adopts the protective paternal role, saving young Frank from the fire while the boy's own father sleeps nearby, befuddled by wine.[13] This action establishes him as "quite one of the family" and wins Esmond the sense of belonging that he has always craved.

His security is dispelled abruptly by Rachel's savage repudiation in the prison scene after the duel, this loss of the maternal figure coming hard on the heels of the death of the paternal figure. But Esmond can survive Rachel's rejection because Castlewood's death has provided him with a crucial step in his process of self-discovery. The secret of his legitimacy has given Esmond important knowledge about who he is and a new sense of self-confidence, so that when Rachel attacks him, "he had to bear him up, at once the sense of his right and the feeling of his wrongs, his honour and his misfortune" (bk. 2. ch. 1). Esmond's experience in prison is an ordeal analogous to the epic hero's trip to the underworld: an introduction to the dark mysteries of life and a ritual test on the way to adulthood or leadership.[14] Esmond himself certainly thinks of it "as an initiation before entering into life—as our young Indians undergo tortures silently before they pass to the rank of warriors in the tribe" (bk. 2, ch. 1). Isolated from the world in his cell, brooding over Rachel's injustice, it seems to Esmond "as if he lived years in that prison and was changed and aged when he came out of it." The whole episode, incorporating as it does his learning the secret of his birth and the end of his adolescent relationship with Rachel, constitutes Esmond's coming of age. He is now ready, as he puts it, to "make a name for myself" and to do so he enters the adult world of war.

But his search for his origins is not quite complete. After his release from prison Esmond rides out to the village where he had lived as a very young boy before he came to Castlewood only to find that the members of his foster family are either dead or gone. Revealing the motive for his journey, he asks himself: "Who was his mother? What had her name been? When did she die?" (bk. 2, ch. 4). This knowledge does not come to him until he meets that keeper of secrets, Father Holt. Holt details the history of Gertrude Maes, the deserted wife and mother who gave up her child to enter a convent. Esmond responds to the story without bitterness, and his search for his roots comes to a symbolic end one spring evening when he visits the convent graveyard where his mother lies buried. This peaceful, secluded spot ("beyond the cemetery walls you had glimpses of life and the world") offers Esmond a moment of meditation outside the ordinary course of life. His turn inward and downward, touching psychic depths, is captured in the haunting image with which he concludes his account: "I felt as one who had been walking below the sea, and treading amidst the bones of shipwrecks" (bk. 2, ch. 13). In the graveyard where the dead intermingle with the organic life of the season ("gentle daisies springing out of the grass") Esmond rededicates himself to life: "I took a little flower off the hillock, and kissed it, and went my way, like the bird that had just lighted on the cross by me, back into the world again" (bk. 2, ch. 13).

Henry Esmond and History

Esmond's private story is entangled in public event; his own history is part of the wider history of his time. More than earlier Thackerayan heroes, Esmond participates in that public life of a nation that we usually call history. He fights in England's wars, engages in its political struggles. His own shift of allegiance from Stuart to Hanover mirrors the same shift in the nation which repudiated with the Stuarts a monarchy supported by divine right, replacing it with a constitutional monarchy supported by Parliament. Esmond himself in fact goes further than does England in rejecting his original conservatism. After years in Virginia ("a land that is independent in all but the name"), he has come to identify himself with a new order, foreseeing and approving the coming American Revolution. "Will we of the new world," he asks, "submit much longer, even nominally, to this antient British superstition [of patching up versus building anew]? There are signs of the times which make me think that ere long we shall care as little about King George here . . . as we do for King Canute or the Druids" (bk. 3, ch. 5). Thackeray will explore the consequences of Esmond's position a few years later in his portrayal of the American struggle for Independence in *The Virginians* (1857–59), his sequel to *Henry Esmond.*

Informing *Henry Esmond* is the liberal or Whig interpretation of English history associated with Thomas Babington Macaulay, whom Thackeray admired and whose popular, multi-volume *History of England from The Accession of James II* (1848–1861) he thought seriously of finishing when Macaulay died leaving his project incomplete.[15] The Whig view is characterized by a belief in history as progress, a belief dependent on a reading of the events of 1688 as the Glorious Revolution. The famous opening of Macaulay's *History* focuses immediately on this revolution which deposed the absolutist House of Stuart and "bound up together the rights of the people and the title of the reigning dynasty." By affirming the principle of a constitutional and Protestant monarch, the settlement of 1688 became for Whigs the cornerstone of the modern British nation, the foundation for all its achievements and progress. Macaulay saw it as generating "a prosperity of which the annals of human affairs had furnished no example," turning England from "a state of ignominious vassalage" into an "umpire among European powers." For him "the history of our country during the last hundred and sixty years is eminently the history of physical, of moral, and of intellectual improvement." Images of rising and growing reinforce such direct statements of the confidence inherent in the progressivist Whig model of history.[16]

Thackeray's innate skepticism denied him Macaulay's confidence, but *Henry Esmond* shares the positive view of 1688, enshrining William of Orange ("wisest" and "bravest" sovereign) and denigrating the Stuarts on whose inept behalf so much fidelity, courage, and blood were "bootlessly expended" (bk. 2, ch. 3). "Were my time to come over again," Esmond states, "I would be a Whig in England and not a Tory" (bk. 3, ch. 5). Despite such assertions, however, Esmond really lacks faith in political process or party and comes to regard English history as a shoddy "series of compromises." Neither Thackeray nor his hero is capable of the kind of historical optimism supporting Macaulay. To Esmond time is circular rather than progressive, and political controversy reveals that all sides are guilty of contradiction and dubious actions. The Glorious Revolution may have been necessary and largely positive, but in the end Esmond gives up on English history, rejecting it for the new history of the New World.[17]

Henry Esmond is a significant historical novel as much for its meditation on historiography as for its interpretation of the past. Thackeray is well aware that our word "history" refers both to what has happened and to the record what has happened, including event and the narrative of event under one rubric. Such conflation is entirely fitting, for the record is crucial; without it, there is in effect no history. But the conflation also underlines the problematic nature of written history which can never correspond to the density of actual event. "Narrative is *linear*," Thomas Carlyle observed, "Action is solid." As a result, "it is not in acted, as it is in written History: actual events are nowise so simply related to each other as parent and offspring are; every single event is the offspring not of one, but of all other events."[18]

Such problems deeply concerned the Victorians who inherited a world where the disappearance of God left only human history as a source of meaning. "To comprehend anything human, be it personal or collective," José Ortega y Gasset has stated, "one must tell its history."[19] Ortega's insight is essentially a nineteenth-century insight, product of an age whose important theories, from the philosophy of Georg W. F. Hegel to the biology of Charles Darwin, were theories of history. To think at all in this period was to think historically, and this had its impact on novels as well. Only in the nineteenth century, George Lukacs argues, did the novel recognize "the specifically historical, that is, derivation of the individuality of characters from the historical peculiarity of their age."[20] To understand a person, one no longer invoked timeless, abstract categories or supernatural forces but turned to the concrete influence of a specific time and place. A static world-view gave way to a dynamic one stressing process; hence, the flourishing of forms like the *Bildungsroman*. In all areas the historical way of thinking became the dominant mode of thought, and historical study itself gained a new preeminence. Carlyle was once again reflecting (if exaggerating) his age when he intoned: "History is not only the fittest study, but the only study, and includes all others whatsoever."[21]

Given this kind of significance and prestige, historical writing came under scrutiny; its authority and objectivity were questioned by minds like that of Thackeray, acutely aware of the subjectivity of truth and the relativity of knowledge. Addressing the muse of history in his lecture on Richard Steele, Thackeray declared: "O venerable daughter of Mnemosyne, I doubt every single statement you ever made since your ladyship was a Muse!" (*The English Humourists*).

Henry Esmond embodies the skepticism beneath that playfulness, placing in doubt the authority of its own hero as historian. Thackeray supplements Esmond's narrative by a series of footnotes by members of the family commenting on and qualifying Esmond's interpretation. A note by the grandsons, for example, suggests that his hatred of the Duke of Marlborough (the English military hero depicted throughout the novel as corrupt and ruthlessly ambitious) was motivated by a personal grudge and fed by unreliable sources (bk. 2, ch. 15). Such qualifications are supported by the self-conscious voice of Esmond himself who raises directly the question of his own reliability in relation to the same Marlborough, admitting that "very likely a private pique of his own may be the cause of his ill-feeling." The distortion of "private pique," however, is but a specific manifestation of the more general problem of perspective in interpretation which Esmond goes on to pose: "We have but to change the point of view, and [the] greatest action looks mean; as we turn the perspective-glass, and a giant appears a pigmy. You may describe, but who can tell whether your sight is clear or not, or your means of information accurate?" (bk. 2, ch. 10).

The entire novel does not rest on such uneasy procedures, but Thackeray includes moments of extreme skepticism like this one to ensure the reader's continuing alertness and to establish that his own novel is subject to the same probing and questioning as the narratives criticized within the fiction. In *Henry Esmond*'s deflation of historical assumptions and procedures (such as the role of the heroic individual and the assumption of objective truth) Esmond himself functions as critic as well as target, sounding the critical note immediately in a Prologue which recalls earlier Thackerayan attacks on sham like *The Book of Snobs*. Angered that history concentrates on kings and courts ignoring "the affairs of the common people," Esmond punctures the myth of royalty by juxtaposing the official version of France's Louis XIV ("the type and model of king-hood") with the unheroic reality of "a little wrinkled old man, pock-marked, and with a great periwig and red heels to make him look tall." England's own Queen Anne is similarly demystified, her official statue set beside a personal glimpse of the queen chasing her hunting dogs: "a hot, red-faced woman. . . . neither better bred nor wiser than you and me." Introducing the realist perspective, Esmond declares, "I would have History familiar rather than heroic," and urges history to "rise up off her knees, and take a natural posture." Fiction, he implies, has long since done so and accordingly provides a "better idea of the manners of the present age in England" than more official records.[22] Distinctions between fiction and history tend to dissolve as their rival narratives cross over into each other's territory. Such blurring, of course, is precisely the function of a historical novel like *Henry Esmond* which wishes to raise questions about the nature of historical knowledge.

Aware of his responsibility to reveal the truth as far as he knows it, Thackeray (through Esmond) attacks most severely the kind of history and fiction where the blurring is a deliberate erasure of a known reality. The main culprit here is military history and the art subservient to it. Esmond's challenge of the accepted heroic image of Marlborough signals a general exposure of the shams of military history. At one point Esmond witnesses "our troops entering the enemy's territory, and putting all round them to fire and sword; burning farms, wasted fields, shrieking women, slaughtered sons and fathers, and drunken soldiery, cursing and carousing in the midst of tears, terrors, and murder." "Why," he stops to ask, "does the stately Muse of History, that delights in describing the valour of heroes and the grandeur of conquest, leave out these scenes, so brutal, mean, and degrading, that yet form by far the greater part of the drama of war?" (bk. 2, ch. 9). By glossing over such realities, the muse of history propagates a false idea of military glory, an idea which Esmond imagines animating many of his readers. Turning to these "gentlemen" and "pretty maidens" who delight in the triumph of war, he asks whether they ever consider the sordidness and brutality that "go to make up the amount of the triumph you admire, and form part of the duties of the heroes you fondle?" (bk. 2, ch. 9).

But Esmond's most devastating attack is reserved for Joseph Addison whose poem *The Campaign* (1705), commemorating the English victory at Blenheim (1704), earned him an official post and marked the end of his poverty. In the novel Esmond meets Addison when he is working on the poem. Upon reading the bland lines whitewashing a "bloody and ruthless part of our campaign," Esmond tells Addison sarcastically: "I admire your art: the murder of the campaign is done to military music, like a battle at the opera, and the virgins shriek in harmony, as our victorious grenadiers march into their villages." His sarcasm soon yields to urgent question and denunciation: "Do you know what a scene it was? . . . . What a triumph you are celebrating? . . . . You hew out of your polished verses a stately image of smiling victory; I tell you 'tis an uncouth, distorted, savage idol; hideous, bloody, and barbarous" (bk. 2, ch. 11). Addison, puffing placidly on his pipe, cites the rules of art and the poet's duty to celebrate the actions of heroes. He finishes his poem and gets his job.

In Joseph Addison and the Duke of Marlborough Esmond has seen important national figures from a closer perspective and found them disappointing. So, also, with the Stuart prince, James Edward, who amply illustrates Esmond's early definition of the Stuarts as a "thankless and thriftless race" (Prologue). Like Queen Anne in the Prologue, all reveal themselves as "neither better bred nor wiser than you and me." Esmond's excursion into the making of English history has been a drama of disillusionment. History as event and history as record both leave him disenchanted.

Patterns of Disenchantment

A similar pattern of disenchantment, identifying maturity with a necessary disillusionment, also pervades Esmond's private history. The young Esmond has a capacity for worship, for creating heroes, that is modified radically as he learns to see clearly and to stand independently. In both the private and public sphere Esmond's sense of self is tied up with the fall of heroes.

His crucial rejection of tradition, signaled by the repudiation of the Stuart cause, has its formal, public expression in Esmond's breaking of the sword before James Edward. But the gesture is informed by its more significant private counterpart—the end of Esmond's passion for Beatrix. "His love of ten years was over;" we are told, "it fell down dead on the spot" (bk. 3, ch. 13). This particular conclusion is itself the culmination of a long process of emotional and moral education that has exposed the hollowness of those whom Esmond has set up as idols. Father Holt, for example, the revered father figure of childhood, turns out to be fallible, self-deceived, even comic in his pretension to significance and secret knowledge. When the adult Esmond reencounters the priest, "he smiled to think that this was his oracle of early days; only now no longer infallible or divine" (bk. 2, ch. 13). As the worship of Beatrix is more serious, so its collapse is more severe. The radiant beauty at whose feet Esmond had knelt and declared, "If you will be Pope, I will turn Papist" (bk. 3, ch. 2), now withers before his eyes: "The roses had shuddered out of her cheeks; her eyes were glaring; she looked quite old" (bk. 3, ch. 13). Beatrix hisses at Esmond like a serpent, fixing him with a killing glance, but her power over him has gone.

This realization of Beatrix's deathly nature prepares Esmond to recognize Rachel who has long loved him patiently and hopelessly. But his new relationship with "the tender matron" is possible only because here, too, Esmond has been disenchanted. To the solitary twelve-year-old boy Rachel appeared a goddess. Golden hair shining in the sun ("a golden halo"), eyes "lighting up," and lips "blooming," she comes upon him in the first scene of the novel "as a *Dea certè.*" The phrase from Virgil is the exclamation of Aeneas ("surely a goddess") when he first sees his mother, Venus, and the classical reference combines with the Christian imagery of haloes to turn Rachel into a type of erotic angel infinitely superior to the enchanted boy. Four-year-old Beatrix underlines the nature of the relationship when she announces: "[Esmond] is saying his prayers to mamma" (bk. 1, ch. 1).

The first crack in this divinity appears when Esmond brings home smallpox after visiting Nancy Sievewright, and Rachel turns on him in a mixture of fear and jealous rage. She later apologizes, but the sun-drenched beatific vision now gives way to a more mundane image as Esmond watches "the taper lighting up her marble face, her scarlet lip quivering, and her shining golden hair" (bk. 1, ch. 8). Rachel herself must encounter disillusionment in her marriage. Her husband finds her adulation of him, her "devotional ceremonies," increasingly irksome and after smallpox mars her beauty, he looks elsewhere for sexual satisfaction. Rachel discovers that her erstwhile god is but "a clumsy idol," her emotional commitment a mere "foolish fiction of love and reverence" (bk. 1, chs. 9, 11). Unconsciously, she comes to love Esmond, the pressure of this unacknowledged, guilty passion exploding in her vehement attack on him in prison after the death of her husband. Shocked by her accusations, Esmond experiences a dramatic inversion of his childhood image of Rachel: "this good angel whom he had loved and worshipped—stood before him, pursuing him with keen words and aspect malign" (bk. 2, ch. 1).

Whether angel or demon, however, Rachel is still somehow suprahuman and therefore alien. Not till the reconciliation a year later in Winchester Cathedral does Esmond see her as fully human: "goddess now no more, for he knew of her weaknesses . . . but more fondly cherished as woman perhaps than ever she had been adored as divinity" (bk. 2, ch. 6). Idealization does continue—the dominant model for their relationship is that between a knight and his lady—but the plane is now a thoroughly human one. Through suffering, Rachel is humbled and brought decisively to earth. Not only does she have to contend for years with a secret passion, she is also forced to act as Esmond's confidante in his love for Beatrix. With the loss of that love Esmond declares that "the drama of my own life was ended" (bk. 3, ch. 13). "Drama" here signifies illusion but also adventure and excitement. Marriage with Rachel, it seems, is what happens when the possibility of drama is over.

But even as Esmond demystifies those around him, he mystifies himself. Among all the "toppling idols," Juliet McMaster finds, "there is only one, Esmond himself, who retains his pedestal. Often enough he even usurps the pedestals of others as they fall."[23] The most striking instance is Rachel's reversal of their initial relationship late in the novel when she falls on her knees before Esmond after learning of his sacrifice of the title. "Let me kneel," she begs him, "let me kneel, and—and—worship you" (bk. 3, ch. 2). The adored Beatrix proves herself an acute psychologist when she tells Esmond that he would never find satisfaction with her because "I won't worship you, and you'll never be happy except with a woman who will." She shrewdly links Esmond and Rachel, suggesting that her mother would have been the perfect wife for him: "You might have sat, like Darby and Joan, and flattered each other; and billed and cooed like a pair of old pigeons on a perch" (bk. 3, ch. 4). This in effect is what Esmond and Rachel go on to do, although the billing and cooing (as the Preface by their daughter hints) may well have been rather less serene than Esmond would have us suppose. In the final pages of the novel he pays tribute to Rachel ("the truest and tenderest and purest wife ever man was blessed with") as the figure who represents for him "the completion of hope, and the summit of happiness" (bk. 3, ch. 13). Esmond's narrative begins and ends with Rachel, so forming a circle embodying the unity of his life as revealed to him in the acts of remembering and re-creating.

But Esmond's narrative is not quite the whole novel. Thackeray opens up the circle by including the Preface by Rachel Esmond Warrington and footnotes by other family members written years later.[24] These not only provide other views of the hero but place his enclosed, circular narrative back into the linear stream of time. Although Esmond himself writes as if his life were over and finally understood, the additions, particularly the one by his daughter, underline that this pose is a fiction. Esmond's narrative is not his life, no matter how much he may wish it were.

Thackeray's narrative strategies thus reinforce *Henry Esmond*'s dominant concern with interpretation and authority. By placing the second Rachel's clearly biased account of her father first in the narrative sequence, Thackeray immediately alerts us to the problem of interpretation. This Rachel reveals herself as self-deceived and father-obsessed, suffering from the same possessiveness that she condemns in her mother ("her jealousy even that my father should give his affection to any but herself"). Blind to any perspective but her own, she is blithely unaware that she is exposing her adored parent, who "never forgave" a tipsy gentleman for "taking a liberty with him" and who "liked to be first in his company" (Preface). Her decisive voice sounds again in the scattered footnotes where the grandsons and the first Rachel also take their turns as commentators, questioning Esmond as autobiographer as well as historian.

No single note presents a serious challenge; no voice emerges as more authoritative than Esmond's own. But their cumulative effect is crucial. By surrounding Esmond's narrative with voices embodying partial and subjective perspectives, Thackeray reminds us that the same limitations inhere in the voice of his narrator-hero. Even within the central narrative, he has Esmond turn on himself on occasion to speculate about the presence of subtle and secret inner motives obscured by the apparent clarity of surface and action. He recognizes, for example, that in renouncing his title he is "perhaps secretly vain of the sacrifice he had made, and to think that he, Esmond, was really the chief of his house, and only prevented by his own magnanimity from advancing his claim" (bk. 2, ch. 3). Such admissions may be disarming, but they nevertheless raise questions about the psychology of Esmond that threaten his moral status as hero. On the one hand, we have the modest portrayal of a man tested by the hard realities of life who grows in wisdom and who proves his selflessness and loyalty; on the other, we have a devious exercise in self-glorification.

The complex, ironic lights moving over the portrait of Esmond preclude a simple choice. Both possibilities must remain open and may be true. Esmond's voice has authenticity and insight, but in Thackeray's world no one voice can have certain authority. The reader is left in disequilibrium, having undergone—like the hero himself—a process of disenchantment.

Chapter Six

The Way of the World: *The Newcomes*

After the experiment of *Henry Esmond* Thackeray returned in his next novel to serial publication and to the world of his own time. *The Newcomes* (1853–55) is the longest and richest of his fictions, a panoramic social novel unfolding leisurely month by month over a period of two years, its characters becoming so familiar to Victorian readers that the *Times*'s review could open with the statement: "Of course we all know the Newcomes."[1] Thackeray himself, in reporting the completion of the novel, stressed its peculiar reality and intimacy for him: "I wrote the last lines . . . with a very sad heart . . . I was quite sorry to part with a number of kind people with whom I had been living and talking these 20 months past" (*Letters*, 3:459).

As usual with Thackeray, however, the beginning of creation was marked by depression and discouragement. In August 1853 he reported gloomily of the new book: "It's not good. It's stupid. It haunts me like a great stupid ghost" (*Letters*, 3:299). Although his confidence in the work grew, the entire novel was written under difficulties, for Thackeray was traveling constantly and was frequently ill. He had to cope not only with his own failing health but also with that of his daughters, both of whom fell ill when on a European tour with their father. In March 1854 he offered the following wry summary of the pressures under which he had been working: "Three illnesses of my own and two of my girls, and four numbers of Newcomes and a Christmas book written in 3 months—I think I have had enough to do" (*Letters*, 3:355). All the more impressive, therefore, are the control and serenity of the novel he produced, a novel Thackeray finally came to regard highly, declaring, "I can't jump further than I did in the Newcomes" (*Letters*, 3:619n).

Victorian readers tended to agree, and *The Newcomes* was regarded widely as Thackeray's masterpiece. Gordon Ray has pointed out that in this novel Thackeray "removed the last obstacle that prevented the great public from taking him to its heart" by creating the endearing figure of the unworldly Colonel Newcome.[2] Such a figure exonerated Thackeray from the charges of cynicism that had been directed routinely at his fiction, reassuring readers that the novelist was capable of imagining and celebrating goodness and simplicity. Reviewers agreed in singling out the Colonel, the *Times* defining him as "a noble creation," while Margaret Oliphant in *Blackwood's Magazine* announced more forcefully: "There has never been a nobler sketch than that of the Colonel."[3] But the "noble" Colonel is no moral paradigm; on the contrary, he is a thoroughly human figure bewildered by the confusions of human existence who stumbles and falls and recovers. Thackeray himself never idealized his character and indeed frequently found the Colonel tiresome and irritating. When his presence in the novel became inhibiting, Thackeray sent him off to India (and out of the novel) for an extended period, remarking that the "story seems to breathe freely after the departure of the dear old boy" (*Letters,* 3:350). At the same time, he revered and loved the "dear old boy," writing for him one of the most moving death scenes in the English novel.[4] Animated by a complex authorial perspective, Colonel Newcome gains depth and resonance, standing as one of the few memorable "good" characters in prose fiction where the heroes of darkness have traditionally been more compelling than those of light.

The Newcomes and the Quixotic Novel

The pictorial capital to Chapter 66 of *The Newcomes* represents Colonel Newcome as Don Quixote, so translating into visual emblem the verbal allusions to the celebrated Knight of La Mancha scattered throughout the text. The Cervantine reference locates the Colonel as a quixotic hero and places the novel within the tradition of quixotic fiction.[5] In a sense, of course, Cervantes' famous work (published in two parts, 1605 and 1615) underlies all novels, Ortega y Gasset arguing that "every novel bears *Quixote* within it like an inner filigree."[6] As a genre, the novel typically demonstrates the hostility of reality to idealisms of all sorts, so following the pattern set by Cervantes, but a quixotic novel features an unworldly, often bookish hero who may be deluded but whose benevolent spirit grants him a certain moral authority. Colonel Newcome clearly fits the type with his generous but weak grasp of reality, his old-fashioned code of the gentleman, and his reliance on texts from the previous century. Since quixotic heroes generally suffer from a disorder of the imagination, the

The Newcomes: pictorial capitals in the chivalric mode

Colonel Newcome as Don Quixote, ch. 66

Clive Newcome as St. George, ch. 56

The election contest between the Colonel and Barnes Newcome, ch. 69

plot containing them consists of one primary action repeated in several variations: the confrontation of the hero's model of reality and reality itself. Accordingly, in *The Newcomes,* as R. D. McMaster has noted, we have a world characterized by a "perpetual tension between the ordering imagination and the resisting raw material of life."[7]

This tension is established dramatically in the first episode of the novel which introduces Colonel Newcome, lately returned to England after thirty-five years in India. The Colonel brings his adolescent son, Clive, to the Cave of Harmony, a tavern famed in the Colonel's youth as the haunt of wits. The wits are long gone, replaced by a more ribald group, but the Colonel characteristically fails to take into account the passage of time. When the odd, archaic figure walks into the Cave, trailing his embarrassed son, the first impulse of the assembled drinkers is mockery, but the Colonel's "stately and polite manner" subdues the laughter, and the company soon responds to the spontaneity of his emotions and to "something touching in the *naiveté* and kindness of the placid and simple gentleman" (ch. 1). Singing sentimental old songs and telling innocent jokes, those present turn the Cave into an embodiment of the Colonel's ideal of genial society. But such transformations can be only temporary. The drunken Captain Costigan begins a "tipsy howl," shattering the illusion and returning the Cave to its normal and—for the Colonel— unbearable state. The atmosphere turns sour; amid uncomfortable sneers, the old soldier stalks out with his son.

Before he does so, he turns on Costigan and delivers a speech identifying the sources of his own code: "Do you dare, sir, to call yourself a gentleman, and to say that you hold the King's commission, and to sit down amongst Christians and men of honour, and defile the ears of young boys with this wicked balderdash?" (ch. 1). The allegiance here is to the British tradition of the officer and gentleman with its vaguely Christian underpinnings and its medieval chivalric roots.[8] Colonel Newcome is less medieval, however, than neoclassical, drawing primarily on the literature of the eighteenth century for sustenance, venerating as "the greatest of men" that portly symbol of neoclassicism, Samuel Johnson (ch. 4). His idea of the gentleman is represented by two eighteenth-century figures, Addison's Sir Roger de Coverley (*Spectator*) and Richardson's Sir Charles Grandison (in the novel of the same name) as well as by Cervantes' seventeenth-century Don Quixote. These three, the Colonel maintains, are "the finest gentlemen in the world" (ch. 4).[9]

The three literary heroes have been his companions through the years, companions nourishing the mind and spirit of a man whose life has been marked by isolation and disappointment: a lonely and severe childhood; an adolescence scarred by an unfulfilled love; an adulthood passed in India far from his only child and his own culture. Increasingly, the Colonel has come to sustain himself by his imagination, figuring forth to himself in the long years of military service how his son will develop and how he and Clive will live together upon his return. His fantasies are fictions woven out of loneliness, ways of rendering bearable the solitude of the present by contemplating anticipated communion in the future. And his dreams for Clive are but part of a larger dream of community, a quixotic dream, for the Colonel's idea of community no longer corresponds (if it ever did) to the way of the world in contemporary England. By bringing a figure like the Colonel into the bourgeois, materialistic world of mid-Victorian England, Thackeray can explore both the realities of society and the unrealities inherent in the models constructed by the human imagination.

Not all is disappointment for Colonel Newcome. Clive is a joy to his father—attractive, lively, generous—and Clive, in turn, is delighted with the Colonel. But other family reunions are less satisfying. The Colonel's two successful half-brothers, Sir Brian Newcome and Hobson Newcome (who run the Newcome banking house), are too caught up in finance and in establishing their social image to care for the unconventional relative they hardly remember. Sir Brian patterns himself after the "Portrait of a Gentleman" at the art gallery ("dignified in attitude, bland, smiling, and statesmanlike"), while Hobson affects the bluff country squire (ch. 6). The Colonel's eldest nephew and heir to the banking concern, Barnes New-come, is more sinister, hiding a mean and ambitious spirit under the pose of a languid young man of fashion. When the Colonel bursts eagerly into their office, he meets with a cool response: "Poor Thomas Newcome was quite abashed by this strange reception. Here was a man, hungry for affection, and one relation asked him to dinner next Monday, and another invited him to shoot pheasants at Christmas" (ch. 6). After a grand dinner at Sir Brian's later in the novel, the Colonel sums up the impoverishment of the Newcome world when he remarks, "I scarcely had enough to eat" (ch. 12).

The women of the family include Hobson's wife, Maria Newcome, who prides herself on her virtue and on her status as a plain merchant's wife ("We are but merchants; we seek to be *no more,*" ch. 8) while all the time consumed with transparent envy of her aristocratic sister-in-law, Lady Ann. Maria greets the Colonel with condescension and dirty gloves. Lady Ann is rather more gracious, impressed by the Colonel's good manners. "The Colonel is perfect," she tells her daughter. "What can Barnes mean by ridiculing him? I wish Barnes had such a distinguished air; but he is like his poor dear papa. *Que voulez-vous,* my love? The Newcomes are honourable, the Newcomes are wealthy; but distinguished? no" (ch. 15). While the frank worldliness of such chatter may be refreshing after the insincere platitudes of Maria Newcome, the passage points to the shallowness underlying Lady Ann's good nature and to the purely social view of human existence which limits her perception. More formidable is her mother, Lady Kew (sister of the Lord Steyne of *Vanity Fair*), who tyrannizes over her unmarried daughter, Lady Julia, and behaves with deliberate rudeness to the Colonel and Clive. She and Barnes Newcome establish themselves early as the hostile forces in the novel, their actions motivated by enmity rather than mere selfishness or indifference.

The Colonel meets Lady Ann and her family by chance at Brighton where he has gone to visit his dead wife's sister, Martha Honeyman. Martha, to whom the word "gentlewoman" is the most admirable in the English language, runs a guest house but remembers always that she is a parson's daughter. Concern with her status does not prevent Martha from being a "good old lady," fond of Clive and loyal to her humbug of a brother, Charles Honeyman, currently a fashionable London preacher making his way through skillful manipulation of a glib tongue and a certain erotic appeal. At Martha Honeyman's the Colonel finds Ethel Newcome, daughter of Lady Ann and heroine of the novel. At thirteen, the dark-haired Ethel is a strong-willed, vivacious creature, her inner warmth often masked by a haughty air adopted to disguise her insecurity. Because of her mother's propensity for changing governesses, Ethel has been badly educated and regards herself as "a monster of ignorance" compared to others of her age (ch. 10). Her self-consciousness is increased by her height which makes her feel "as if every one stared" when she walks with her contemporaries (ch. 10). Accordingly, she takes refuge in imperious behavior and in the society of small children. But the Colonel touches her. He and Ethel "fell in love with each other instantaneously," she responding to his kind spirit and he seeing in her the beloved Léonore he lost forty years ago (ch. 15). With memories of Léonore rekindled, the Colonel now fantasizes a romantic future for Clive and Ethel.

At the moment, however, Clive finds the high-spirited Ethel "a very haughty, spoiled, aristocratic young creature" (ch. 20) and concentrates on enjoying the sensations of leaving school, growing a moustache, and studying art at Gandish's academy with his friend, J. J. Ridley. More talented than Clive, J. J. is socially and physically inferior and worships the handsome and fortunate youth whom he regards as his patron.

Accepting the worship, Clive nevertheless acknowledges—and proclaims—that J. J.'s imagination is richer and more powerful than his own. Clive's pleasure-loving nature makes the discipline of art irksome and he soon arranges his person more carefully than his drawing. While the son explores the new world of adulthood, the father rushes around England visiting friends and acquaintances. "Having nothing whatever to do," the narrator comments, "our Colonel's movements are of course exceedingly rapid" (ch. 15).[10]

As such narrative comments suggest, there is an emptiness in the Colonel's life. His good friend, James Binnie, observing the Colonel's restlessness and increasingly gaunt appearance, declares that "Newcome had grown older in three years in Europe, than in a quarter of a century in the East" (ch. 21). Longing to share his son's life, the Colonel must face the inevitable gap between generations. When he joins a lively gathering of Clive and his friends, a sudden hush ensues; when they discuss literature, their disrespect for his revered eighteenth century seems to the Colonel "rank blasphemy"; when they talk about art, their language is to him incomprehensible. The Colonel tries to understand, reading the new poets and gazing at the admired sculptures "desperately praying to comprehend them, and puzzled before them" (ch. 21). The aesthetic views of the young men not only bewilder the Colonel but shake his neoclassic confidence in the existence of permanent truths: "If the young men told the truth, where had been the truth in his own young days?" (ch. 21). Painfully, he realizes that though he and Clive are together, "yet he was alone still." He decides to return to India "where I have some friends, and where I am somebody still" (ch. 26).

After his departure, the focus of the novel shifts to Clive, and Thackeray translates the quixotic theme of the clash between real and ideal into the terms of a courtship novel, exposing the cynicism of the marriage market in the Newcome world. Clive and J. J. Ridley set off for a tour of Europe, supposedly to pursue their artistic education. J. J. does draw, but Clive falls in love when he unexpectedly runs into Ethel on her way to Baden with part of her family. They spend an idyllic few weeks before Barnes and Lady Kew arrive to shatter the holiday mood. Unconstrained by their severe presence, Ethel has bloomed, her fresh beauty and sparkling spirit enchanting Clive. But Clive is a social inferior; moreover, Ethel is reputedly promised to her cousin, Lord Kew, their marriage a long-cherished dream of old Lady Kew.

Clive's untenable position is brought home to him by the story of Clara Pulleyn. Daughter of an impoverished nobleman with many daughters,

Clara fell in love with Jack Belsize, profligate younger son of Lord Highgate. The family interfered in so unprofitable a courtship, and the unhappy Clara is now engaged to Barnes Newcome, the two families congregating at Baden to conclude the agreement. The unexpected appearance of Belsize (at sight of whom Clara faints) creates an uproar; even the generous Lord Kew is incensed at the behavior of Belsize, a close friend. Clive takes the lesson to heart, deciding to retreat even before Lady Kew announces coldly that Ethel's engagement to Kew "has long been settled in our family" (ch. 30). Taking the disconsolate Belsize with them, Clive and J. J. leave for Rome.

At Baden Ethel behaves capriciously, engaging in outbursts of temper and treating with scorn even the inoffensive Lord Kew, who is understandably puzzled and hurt by her "wanton ill humour" (ch. 32). Bitter and unhappy at her participation in the marriage market which has cost her the loving Clive and replaced him with a man whose affection seems mild, Ethel rages against society for being "unblushingly sordid" (ch. 32). Doing her best to provoke Kew, she deliberately embarrasses him at a ball by playing the dazzling coquette. When he comes to remonstrate with her the next morning, she silences his "sermon" by showing him a letter she has just received from one of his former lovers (the Duchesse d'Ivry) detailing his own less-than-respectable behavior in the past. Realizing that Ethel does not love him, Kew signals his renunciation by kissing her hand; Ethel "never liked him so much as at that moment" (ch. 34). Shortly afterwards, Kew becomes unwillingly involved in a quarrel engineered by the jealous Duchesse d'Ivry and fights a duel during which he is wounded.

In Rome Clive begins to recover from his disappointment about Ethel until a chance meeting with the convalescent Lord Kew informs him of the broken engagement and sends his hopes soaring. He rushes immediately to England but finds access to Ethel difficult. She is the reigning beauty of the season, and Lady Kew, determined on a great catch, has her eye on the rich if semimoronic Marquis of Farintosh. When Clive does manage to sneak a private meeting with Ethel, she tells him: "Neither you nor I can alter our conditions, but must make the best of them" (ch. 41). Despite the lack of hope, Clive continues his pursuit of Ethel whose treatment of him is now warm now brittle, now playful now haughty. In the background of Clive's life stands Rosey Mackenzie, niece of the Colonel's old friend, James Binnie, and daughter of the formidable Mrs. Mackenzie whose smiling exterior conceals a cold and scheming interior. Dominated by her mother, Rosey is but a pretty cipher, her bland personality offering no competition to the fascinating Ethel.

After three years in India, where he has become a rich man and director of the Bundelcund Bank, Colonel Newcome returns to England. He finds Sir Brian dead and Barnes in his place, Lady Kew in virtual control of Ethel, and Clive suffering from his continuing and hopeless love. No longer so naive, the Colonel this time attempts to enter society on its own terms: he tries to buy Ethel for his son. Without telling Clive, he offers Barnes a substantial financial settlement in return for the hand of Ethel. Barnes informs Lady Kew but not Ethel, and the dowager is outraged: "Lady Kew wondered what the impudence of the world would come to. An artist propose for Ethel!" (ch. 52). Unwilling to lose the business of the Colonel's bank, Barnes lies and keeps Colonel Newcome dangling while Lady Kew pursues Lord Farintosh, who is finally "brought to bay" in Paris. News of Ethel's engagement to Farintosh awakens the Colonel to full realization of Barnes's duplicity, and he accuses him publicly of being "a liar and a cheat" (ch. 53). The Colonel's anger includes Ethel as well, and his anger once aroused is unrelenting. He takes Clive to Europe, leaving Barnes to luxuriate in the prospect of having a sister who is a Marchioness. Wedding plans, however, are interrupted: first, by the death of Lady Kew (whereupon Ethel inherits sixty thousand pounds); and finally, by the disintegration of Barnes's own marriage to Clara. Completely demoralized by her loveless marriage, Clara runs off with her old lover, Jack Belsize (now Lord Highgate), and the shock of Clara's action prompts Ethel to examine her own values and to confront her growing doubts about marriage to Farintosh. She breaks the engagement and devotes herself to caring for Clara's children, but the decision comes too late, for Clive has just married Rosey Mackenzie.

Clive marries to "please the best father in the world" and to "settle that question about marriage and have an end of it" (ch. 62). Not surprisingly, the Colonel is happier with the marriage than the son, adoring his daughter-in-law whose emotional shallowness he fails to perceive. Though simple in his own tastes, he "desired that his children should have the best of everything" (ch. 62). The Colonel buys a sumptuous mansion in Tyburnia, its gaudy furnishings reflecting the decorator's taste and not his own, so emphasizing the erosion of the Colonel's own values in the second half of the novel and his estrangement from the sources of his inner strength. At the mansion he gives splendid banquets, but "in the midst of all these splendours" Clive sits "gaunt, and sad, and silent" (ch. 63). The bank bores him, and so does his wife. To the Colonel, Clive's "evident unhappiness was like a reproach" and his nature sours (ch. 64). Where he had formerly preached Christian forgiveness, he now nurses his vindictive feelings toward Barnes and snubs Ethel. The skirmishes between Barnes and the Colonel develop into a full-scale campaign when they both contest the same parliamentary seat. The Colonel wins, but his victory is marred by disquieting rumors about the bank, by his strained relationship with Clive, and by the disruptive presence of Mrs. Mackenzie who reentered the household when Rosey gave birth to a son.

Soon after the election, the bank collapses, and bankruptcy restores all the Colonel's nobility of character. He behaves with honor and dignity, but he is a broken man, suffering profound guilt at having influenced friends and relatives (like Rosey and Martha Honeyman) to invest in what has turned out to be a fraudulent enterprise. The egregious Mrs. Mackenzie loses no time in accusing him of having "robbed" and "cheated" her darling child, and he must endure not only her constant reproaches but also the knowledge that his beloved Rosey sides with her mother. Clive, on the other hand, is brought closer to his father by the disaster and shaken out of his lethargy. He acts with resolution, moving the family to Boulogne and working long hours at making drawings and giving lessons in order to support them. And all the while he watches his father age rapidly under the tyranny of Mrs. Mackenzie, his wife grow more nervous and hysterical under the influence of her mother. A brief respite ensues when Clive and the Colonel move back to London, a more profitable market for Clive's talents, but Mrs. Mackenzie soon follows and the Colonel flees to Martha Honeyman's. When even the good-natured Martha cannot refrain from alluding "more than once to the fact that her money had been thrown away," the old man flees once more, this time taking refuge in impersonal charity as a pensioner at Grey Friars, the school both he and Clive had attended (ch. 75).

Ethel has been deeply upset by the misfortunes of the Colonel and Clive and has helped them secretly. Now a chance discovery allows her to give more open and substantial assistance. She finds a letter written by the Colonel's stepmother before her death leaving Clive a legacy. When Barnes refuses to honor the letter, Ethel herself makes up the six-thousand-pound bequest as coming from the family. Clive's first thought upon learning of his good fortune is that he can now repay and so rid himself of Mrs. Mackenzie. "Mrs. Mackenzie," he tells her, "I can bear you no more" (ch. 79). The heightened domestic tensions, exacerbated by a visit from Ethel, send the ailing and pregnant Rosey into hysterics. She gives birth to a stillborn baby and dies herself. At the same time, the Colonel drifts toward death. Now reconciled to Ethel, he is comforted by her presence and by the presence of the woman he had loved and lost in his youth, Léonore de

Florac. In a "heart-rending" voice, he calls "Léonore, Léonore" just before he dies, but his final word is "Adsum," the schoolboy response signaling "I am here" when the roll is called (ch. 80). With the death of Colonel Newcome, the main narrative ends. But Thackeray adds a brief epilogue in which he fancies "that in Fable-land somewhere Ethel and Clive are living most comfortably together."

Anatomy of a Respectable Society

The quixotic novel is double-pronged; even as it probes the limitations of the imagination, it questions the reality that defeats our imaginings. And the most immediately obstructive level of reality in *The Newcomes* is social reality, the reality created by the powerful, commercial classes in mid-Victorian England. Their impact is felt throughout the entire social spectrum, touching the divergent worlds of the shabby genteel boarding house and the glittering society ball, the severe Evangelical home and the dissolute gambling casino. But the center is mercantile London where to be a Barnes Newcome is to be a success and where one finds "the most polite, and most intelligent, and best informed, and best dressed, and most selfish people in the world" (ch. 25). The code supporting these people is respectability, and Thackeray draws attention to its centrality in his text by subtitling the novel: "Memoirs of a Most Respectable Family." To Sally Baxter, the young American who was a model for Ethel Newcome, Thackeray defined the London world as "the most godless respectable thing." It is "base and prosperous and content, not unkind—very well bred—very unaffected in manner, not dissolute—clean in person and raiment and going to church every Sunday—but in the eyes of the Great Judge of right & wrong what rank will those people have with all their fine manners and spotless characters and linen?" (*Letters,* 3:297).

Thackeray's indictment of respectability isolates the destructive moral confusion at its root. Respectability, Juliet McMaster has argued, is the "complex union of, or confusion between, financial and moral values, good and goods."[11] Qualitative moral concepts like virtue become materialized into quantitative concepts, located in external forms that can be counted and measured, as Maria Newcome measures—to her own satisfaction—her superior quotient of virtue. The translation of good into goods is illustrated most memorably in the fashionable Lady Whittlesea's chapel where Charles Honeyman purveys his facile religiosity. The chapel rests literally on the wine vaults of Sherrick and Company, and their loans support the running of the religious concern. A cheerful entrepreneur,

Sherrick refers to the chapel as "the shop" and explains his loans by saying "I thought it was a good speculation." To Sherrick all activities are reduced to the same activity: "It's all a speculation. I've speculated in about pretty much everything that's going: in theatres, in joint-stock jobs, in building ground, in bills, in gas and insurance companies, and in this chapel" (ch. 26).

Sherrick, of course, is not quite respectable: such open admission of a thorough commercialism is not genteel. Respectability entails reticence, a public adherence to values of a more intellectual, spiritual, or emotional cast. "Fashion I do not worship," Maria Newcome asserts, ". . . but genius and talent I do reverence" (ch. 8). The system encourages pretense and self-deception, establishing a system of hypocrisy in which Maria Newcomes flourish. It is Maria who prompts the subversive narrative question: "The wicked are wicked no doubt . . . but who can tell the mischief which the very virtuous do?" (ch. 20). Of all the Newcomes, Barnes understands most fully the code of respectability and uses it to his advantage. He attends church, dresses properly, keeps his appointments, and generally maintains a socially inoffensive demeanor. But he is mean-spirited and a domestic tyrant, crushing the spirit of his wife, who rouses herself sufficiently to defy convention and leave him. Society, most notably in the shape of a jury of "respectable" men, rallies around the husband. After hearing accounts of Barnes's brutal treatment of Clara, the jury "consoled the injured husband with immense damages," and so "put money in his pocket for having trampled on the poor weak young thing." Clara, meanwhile, lives as an outcast, scorned by those who are "as criminal but undiscovered" (ch. 58). Not long after the scandal, Barnes delivers a public lecture on the sacredness of the domestic affections.

The elaborate social code of the Newcome world covers over the predatory nature of existence in this society. "To push on in the crowd," the narrator notes, "every male or female struggler must use his or her shoulders" (ch. 8). This observation launches a passage of worldly advice (whose irony resides in its accuracy) developing the insight: "What a man has to do in society is to assert himself." Accordingly, if a "neighbour's foot obstructs you, stamp on it; and do you suppose he won't take it away?" (ch. 8). The predatory theme is announced at the very beginning of the novel in the Overture which presents a mixture of animals from familiar animal fables, all envying one another and jostling for position. Animal imagery persists throughout the text, reinforcing through metaphor the fierceness of the struggle for advantage exposed in narrative action and commentary.[12] Lady Kew is seen as an eagle, hunting down prey for her granddaughter, while Mrs. Mackenzie appears as a boa constrictor ready to swallow her own child. With her mother, Rosey is like a "bird before a boa-constrictor, doomed—fluttering, fascinated" (ch. 73). As for Clara Pulleyn, she is a "poor little fish" whose only "duty" is to be devoured (ch. 28). Such cannibalistic motifs sharpen the predatory theme, identifying the sinister basis for so many of the relationships in this world. The note is sounded in different tones, struck lightly in Ethel's casual remark that "Barnes was ready to kill me and eat me" (ch. 28) and more heavily in the repellent image of society women as "ghouls feasting on the fresh corpse of a reputation" (ch. 31).

Gambling images, moving from literal to metaphoric reference in the chapters on the fashionable resort of Baden, further define the darkness at the heart of society. "Besides roulette and trente-et-quarante," the narrator notes, "a number of amusing games are played at Baden, which are not performed, so to speak, *sur table*" (ch. 28). Thackeray uses the vocabulary of gambling to locate and indict the mercenary impulse that controls the fashionable world:

Here the widow plays her black suit and sets her bright eyes against the rich bachelor, elderly or young, as may be. Here the artful practitioner, who has dealt in a thousand such games, engages the young simpleton with more money than wit. . . . Here mamma, not having money perhaps, but metal more attractive, stakes her virgin daughter against Count Fettacker's forests and meadows; or Lord Lackland plays his coronet, of which the jewels have long since been in pawn, against Miss Bags' three per cents. (ch. 28)

People become only counters in the social game, with mothers staking their virgin daughters and widows and earls staking themselves. All see others—and themselves—in a purely functional light, their definition of an individual depending always on that individual's potential role in the struggle for wealth and status.

Young women, in particular, suffer this debasement, and Thackeray's fiercest attack is directed at the marriage market, "the selling of virgins" which the Newcome world deems necessary to its continuance. The hard edge of Thackeray's condemnation of this practice in the novel may owe something to his apprehension lest his lively, cherished Sally Baxter contract a worldly marriage. Impelled by his concern, he wrote her an impassioned letter (July–August 1853) warning against "money-marriages" which lead to empty lives and to children who "when their turn comes are bought and sold, and respectable and heartless as their parents before them." Such people, he urged, "throttle" love and "fling it under the sewer as poor girls do their unlawful children" (*Letters*, 3:297). The violent language here simultaneously conveys Thackeray's anger and identifies the worldly response to love: love is illegitimate and to be eradicated ruthlessly. So it is with the love of Clara Pulleyn and Jack Belsize in *The Newcomes*. Their love interferes with the plans of their elders who arrange Jack's arrest and subject Clara to relentless pressures that result in her acceptance of a mercenary marriage to Barnes Newcome. The novel stresses that Clara is but a specific example of a general case, an emblem of all the virgins, "offered up to the devouring monster, Mammon" while "respectable female dragons" look on (ch. 58).

Images of tyranny and death mingle with metaphors from commerce to define the marriage market, dominating the novel's most concentrated meditation on the theme (Chapter 28). Here allusions to suttee, the Hindu custom of a widow cremating herself on her husband's funeral pile, link the "orange flowers" of an English society wedding to a sacrificial death rite. For the young women in the marriage market, marriage is a death, their marriage bed a "deadly couch" upon which parents have "thrust" them. "Though I like to walk . . . in an earl's house, splendid, well ordered," the narrator comments, ". . . yet there are times when the visit is not pleasant." One of these times is when "the parents in that fine house are getting ready their daughter for sale, and frightening away her tears with threats, and stupefying her grief with narcotics, praying her and imploring her, and dramming her, and coaxing her, and blessing her, and cursing her." What heightens the immorality of this whole process is the pretense that the mercenary marriage is in fact a marriage of regard. Lady Ann dispatches to Clara "rather a pretty little poem about welcoming the white Fawn to the Newcome bowers," and the Newcomes preserve all the rituals belonging to a less materialistic concept of marriage. When Ethel dramatizes the sordid reality of social practice by coming to dinner with a green "Sold" ticket pinned to her white dress, Lady Kew (chief marriage negotiator) tears the card from her breast in anger at Ethel's frank recognition of her status as commodity (ch. 28).

The marriage market has a pernicious effect on both individuals and society, breeding hypocrisy, unhappy families, and bitter creatures like the Duchesse d'Ivry, married at sixteen to a man past sixty. The gentle Clara becomes "schooled into hypocrisy by tyranny" (ch. 53), while the more aggressive Duchesse lives out fantasies of emotional intensity, taking each lover "through the complete dramatic course,—tragedies of jealousy, pantomimes of rapture, and farces of parting" (ch. 34). Internally hollow, she plays one role after another: she *"was* what she acted" (ch. 34). In this world lives are unreal, distorted, and wasted. And such lives are primarily female lives, for a "young man begins the world with some aspirations at least," whereas a "girl of the world" knows from the beginning that "the object of her existence, is to marry a rich man" (ch. 45). To that end, she is "schooled," instructed that "the article of Faith in her catechism is, 'I believe in elder sons, and a house in town, and a house in the country!' " To prepare women to conform to this shallow credo, society stunts deliberately their natural emotions: "By long cramping and careful process, their little natural hearts have been squeezed up, like the feet of their fashionable little sisters in China." Minds as well as hearts are cramped and squeezed up, a "brave intellect" reduced for its "sole exercise" to hatboxes, scandal, and the "fiddle-faddle etiquette of the Court" (ch. 45). Caught in the respectable world's confusion between good and goods, women are only the most obvious victims of a system whose viciousness lies in its general stultification of the human spirit.

Ethel Newcome and the Victorian Heroine

Ethel Newcome, Thackeray's most complex heroine, both resists and participates in the general stultification of the respectable world. In her ambivalence she represents a significant modification of Victorian convention and a new kind of woman for Thackeray. "Mr. Thackeray is not, for the most part, a flattering painter of women," wrote Thackeray's contemporary, Whitwell Elwin in 1855. "The clever are artful and wicked; the good are insipid. Ethel is a great exception, and has no counterpart in *Vanity Fair* or *Pendennis.*"[13] Perhaps because Ethel has "no counterpart" in his previous fiction, Thackeray's handling of her betrays some uneasiness, particularly when it comes to dealing with Ethel's worldliness. At such points narrative commentary becomes densely entangled in qualification and contradiction as it hesitates among various explanations of her conduct. Throughout the novel Thackeray is acutely aware of her unconventionality as heroine, and his habitual self-consciousness increases whenever her status in the fiction is in question.[14]

The novel continually draws attention to how Ethel evades regular categories and defies the usual expectations about heroines. Pursuing the unworthy Lord Farintosh, for example, she is "in a very awkward position as a heroine," and the narrator threatens playfully that had he "another ready to my hand," he would depose Ethel "at this very sentence" (ch. 45). Underlying the humor is a serious issue: how far can a novelist allow his heroine to break the rules without losing her the sympathy of the reader? Thackeray is acutely aware of what convention permits a heroine. "To break her heart in silence for Tomkins who is in love with another; to suffer no end of poverty, starvation, capture by ruffians, ill-treatment by a bullying husband, loss of beauty by the smallpox, death even at the end of the volume"—all this, the narrator declares, a heroine may "endure" without forfeiting the "sentimental reader's esteem" (ch. 45). So long as she is a passive victim ("to break her heart in silence," "to suffer"), she moves the sensibility of the reader, who appears here as rather a sadistic voyeur. But Thackeray's main point is less the neurosis of the reader than the passivity and loyalty of the domestic heroine, his allusions to smallpox recalling his own long-suffering Rachel Esmond and Dickens's Esther Summerson, the perfect domestic heroine of *Bleak House.*

In contrast to such heroines, Ethel seems unusually aggressive and fickle. A coquette, she enjoys her power over men, and so long as her targets are worldly young men in the marriage market, the reader enjoys her wit and gaiety. But when she flirts with the deeply loving Clive, whom she has no intention of marrying, Ethel risks the reader's sympathy. And Thackeray knows it, devoting a passage of narrative commentary to the problem. Invoking the symbol of British propriety, Mrs. Grundy, the narrator claims to agree with "Mrs. Grundy and most moralists" in finding Ethel's flirtation with Clive "highly reprehensible." He adds in ostensible explanation: "I allow . . . that a virtuous young woman of high principle, etc., etc., having once determined to reject a suitor, should separate from him utterly then and there" (ch. 53). The dismissive "etc., etc." immediately punctures the conventional response, and the narrator in fact goes on to overturn Mrs. Grundy and condone Ethel. Her desire to see Clive, for whom she has a real regard, is "not blameable" because "every flutter which she made to escape out of the meshes which the world had cast about her, was but the natural effort at liberty" (ch. 53). What is wrong with Ethel is rather her worldly "prudence" and "submission" than the impulse drawing her to Clive.

The vitality that seeks to escape the confines of worldly society is expressed in Ethel's dark-haired beauty. She recalls a "beautiful panther" in the zoo, the analogy suggesting something exotic, restless, and potentially dangerous in Ethel (ch. 41). Hers is clearly a sexual beauty (Clive muses often on her fine form), and she is most at ease in uncultivated open spaces or in physical movement, dancing or riding. Clive's infatuation begins appropriately in the mountains when he unexpectedly runs across

Ethel riding a donkey, clad in white with a touch of crimson, carrying a bunch of wild flowers. His artist's eye responds to the play of light and shade that chequers her face and dress with shadow but lingers on "the light . . . all upon her right cheek: upon her shoulder down to her arm, which was of a warmer white, and on the bunch of flowers which she held, blue, yellow, and red poppies, and so forth" (ch 27). Clive's sensuous response recalls the more decorous but equally appreciative response of his father to Ethel as a young girl galloping in the park, black hair and red ribbons flying (ch. 20).

These pastoral images are darkened by allusions to classical and biblical myth which suggest an underlying fierceness and destructiveness. At one point Clive considers Ethel and the blond Rosey Mackenzie as subjects for painting. For Ethel he conjures up the heroic, passionate, and "unfeminine" images of the classical huntress, Diana, and the biblical seductresses, Judith and Salome, whose beauty was deadly. To save her town, Judith seduced the enemy general, Holofernes, and cut off his head; while Salome (daughter of Herodias) enchanted her stepfather, Herod, with her famous dance and requested the head of John the Baptist on a platter as reward. "She would do for Judith, wouldn't she?" Clive exclaims of Ethel. "Or how grand she would look as Herodias's daughter sweeping down a stair . . . holding a charger [platter] before her with white arms, you know—with the muscles accented like that glorious Diana at Paris—a savage smile on her face and a ghastly solemn gory head on the dish" (ch. 25). Where Ethel looms as potentially explosive and threatening, Rosey appears in diminutive imagery as a "little wild flower," "a little child at play," and "a tremulous, fluttering little linnet." Rosey, Clive declares, should be painted "in milk" (ch. 25). Rosey is delicate, vulnerable, and immature; she arouses Clive's protective instincts but neither his imagination nor his desire.

To love Ethel, as Clive learns, is to love a wayward, fierce creature whose aggressive behavior expresses as much internal tension as it does contempt for the world of shams in which she finds herself. Ethel's conflict between accepting and rebelling against worldly values defines her and gives her character its depth. On the one hand, she sees clearly the debased values of the Newcome world ("this severe Diana . . . whose arrows were so keen"), and she reacts by provoking and defying Lord Kew and her grandmother. "We are as much sold as Turkish women," she states bluntly to Lady Kew, and her rage at the "slavery" intimidates even the powerful old lady who "was fairly afraid of her" (ch. 32). Ethel's "high spirit" recalls a young colt, "stubborn in training, rebellious to the whip, and wild under harness" (ch. 33). Since Ethel is spirited enough to reject the world in face of opposition (as she eventually does after Clara's elopement), her long period of worldliness underlines the degree to which she accepts the code in which she has been reared.

She has absorbed many of its values, looking down on artists, for example, as "very good people, but, you know, not *de notre monde*" (ch. 28). When she attempts to persuade Clive to give up art for something more respectable, he accuses her: "you are in the world, you love the world, whatever you may say" (ch. 47). To the gentle and pious Lénore de Florac (herself a victim of the marriage market) Ethel acknowledges the accuracy of Clive's perception: "I who pretend to revolt, I like [society] too; and I, who rail and scorn flatterers—oh, I like admiration" (ch.47). At moments the moral and emotional clarity apparent in her as a child surface to make her "despise" her own baseness and complicity in a hollow system, but self-castigation brings with it no recognition of an alternative: "When I lie in bed, and say I have been heartless and a coquette, I cry with humiliation; and then rebel and say, Why not?" (ch. 47). Until Clara's fate shows her why not, Ethel tries out different roles in an effort to achieve a harmony between inner impulse and outer fact. She enjoys striking poses, as when she yearns aloud for a convent to join or a field to plough, but her uncertainty and turmoil are real enough. Ethel's capricious behavior and brittle chatter are but external signs of an internal conflict generated by a basic confusion about values.

The conventional heroine (like Laura Pendennis) is never confused about values, nor is the conventional antiheroine (like Becky Sharp) who embraces the way of the world. Ethel's originality and interest lie in her falling between the two types. Unlike either Laura or Becky, Ethel is not static but dynamic. She does not spring full-blown upon the first page in which she appears but changes and grows in the course of the novel. Thackeray allows her to experiment with life, to enter the mainstream rather than sit on the sidelines as the domestic heroine tends to do. And her participation in the vanities of existence does not condemn her, as it does a Becky or a Beatrix Esmond, to an immoral and empty life. Through Ethel, Thackeray in effect gives the heroine the same freedom to learn from experience that the Victorian novel traditionally granted the hero, and Ethel is more like the young Arthur Pendennis than she is like Laura Bell. No longer angel or devil, the heroine joins the hero as fallible individual.[15]

Imagination and Daydream

Clive's imagination allows him to grasp something essential about Ethel when he perceives her in the heroic mode, but imagination in *The Newcomes* is more typically the "deceiving elf" of Keats's "Ode to a Nightingale." Clive himself tells Ethel sadly, "it is with their own fancies that men fall in love" (ch. 41). Craving meaning, order, and beauty, the human mind projects patterns onto experience and sets up interpretive fictions. Rarely do such imaginative projections survive the test of actuality. Clive's early fiction of Ethel as "fairy-princess" and himself as her knight crumbles in the face of social reality: "I remember when I thought I would like to be Ethel's knight. . . . I remember when I was so ignorant I did not know there was any difference in rank between us" (ch. 47).[16]

As a quixotic novel *The Newcomes* subjects its fanciful characters to disillusionment. But it is as much concerned with exploring the imaginative drive as with demonstrating the failure of its constructs. Primarily through Colonel Newcome, Thackeray investigates the urge not merely to interpret but to shape and control reality, uncovering in the process the egotism of the imagination in even so generous a creature as the Colonel. His dreams and plans for Clive are dreams of compensation for his own frustrated life; through his son he attempts to rewrite his own story. Where he suffered early exile, sent off to India because of his rebellious behavior, Clive will learn to be "a gentleman in the world" and find the social acceptance that has eluded his father. After the Colonel meets Ethel, the dream takes on an added dimension, for she startles into life memories of his lost Léonore, recalling "a pair of eyes I haven't seen these forty years." Immediately, he begins to form "a fine castle . . . whereof Clive was lord, and that pretty Ethel, lady" (ch. 15). Before his departure for India it is the Colonel, not Clive, who virtually courts Ethel.

The pattern reappears even more strongly with Rosey Mackenzie. Once Ethel seems out of reach, the Colonel substitutes Rosey, he and Binnie scheming "that their young ones should marry and be happy ever after, like the prince and princess of the fairy-tale" (ch. 26). Clive marries to fulfill that dream, though he knows that "happy ever after" will never be his. For a time it seems to be within reach of the Colonel who in effect takes the place of his son, squiring Rosey around London, lavishing presents on her, and insisting on presenting her to royalty. "I think," Laura Pendennis notes shrewdly, "that Colonel Newcome performs all the courtship part of the marriage" (ch. 65). Clive retreats into passivity and depression as time impresses upon him ever more forcefully that he and Rosey "were not made to mate with one another" (ch. 63).

The Colonel's experience suggests that fairy tales are never entirely innocent, that daydreams transposed to reality deform the lives they touch. Watching Clive's misery, the Colonel becomes embittered: "What young man on earth could look for more? a sweet young wife, a handsome home, of which the only encumbrance was an old father, who would give his last drop of blood in his son's behalf. And it was to bring about this end that Thomas Newcome had toiled and had amassed a fortune!" (ch. 63). The note of hurt ego identifies the problem as one of defining the self through dream of another. Whatever good may be intended, the formative impulse is the self-centered one of desire to stamp one's own image on the earth. In this respect both the benevolent Colonel and the malevolent Lady Kew are engaged in the identical activity of ensuring their mark on the shape of the future. Thackeray recognizes the desire as a deeply human one expressing a necessary hope. When the Colonel faces the inevitability of the generational gap between father and son, "he thought what vain egotistical hopes he used to form about the boy" and "a sickening and humiliating sense of the reality came over him" (ch. 21). Without "hopes" reality becomes a matter of despair. Even the imperious Lady Kew falters when she has to confront the failure of her plan to marry her two favorite grandchildren, betraying an uncharacteristic uncertainty: "I don't know. I am an old woman—the world perhaps has changed since my time." The isolation and emotional hunger of this hard old woman surface briefly as she turns to Ethel: "Don't leave me too, my child. Let me have something I can like at my years" (ch. 38). Despite such moments, however, the fact remains that the dreams of Lady Kew and Colonel Newcome (different as they are in important respects) destroy the happiness of Clive and Ethel.

Lady Kew dies thinking that her plan for a brilliant marriage for Ethel has succeeded, but Colonel Newcome lives to see all of his dreams shattered and to learn how "sickening and humiliating" reality can be. In Boulogne he attempts to face an existence rendered unbearable by the constant accusations of Mrs. Mackenzie which only exacerbate his already deep sense of guilt. Having acknowledged not only the folly but the harm of his desire to shape reality to his dreams, the Colonel becomes passive and apologetic, surrendering confidence and control. The sudden stooping of his formerly erect carriage serves as physical analogue for the change within. Restored to virtue and purged of vanity, the Colonel nevertheless remains a quixotic hero to whom reality is unendurable. Images of flight and retreat characterize the final stage of his life as he flees first from Mrs. Mackenzie and then from Martha Honeyman to find refuge in the school of his boyhood. Here the female furies cannot pursue him, and he finds peace in the ordered life of a poor pensioner. As his health fails, time itself becomes blurred and elastic, and his connection with the present weakens. When he dies, he dies as a child with a schoolboy response on his lips.

Only when expressed in art is the activity of the imagination affirmed in *The Newcomes*. But the affirmation is problematic, for the paintings of J. J. Ridley belong to "dreamland" and not to the realist model of art that Thackeray himself espoused. Through the characterization of J. J., Thackeray segregates the imagination from actuality, defuses its potency for transformation. J. J. is born into an uncomprehending, dingy world, and he escapes by dreaming about and re-creating in drawings romance images gleaned from Gothic novels, melodramatic tales, and the stories of Walter Scott. A full-page illustration of "J. J. in Dreamland" (serving also as frontispiece for the novel) repeats in another medium the prose images of love and war that stir J. J.'s imagination (ch. 11). Although Thackeray does make some attempts to present J. J. as a kind of Wordsworthian artist who sees "beauties manifest in forms, colours, shadows of common objects" (ch. 11), he does not push seriously the Wordsworthian role of poet of common life. J. J. continues to be portrayed primarily in romance and fairy-tale motifs which emphasize the separation rather than conjunction of his art and the world of ordinary experience.

J. J. lives in a world apart, able to escape magically the problems of existence. From the beginning Thackeray stresses J. J.'s role as the fortunate youth, allying him with magic by likening his gift to "a charm or a flower which the wizard gives, and which enables the bearer to see the fairies." As a result, J. J. is able to live in the "fair Art-world" and to avoid the "vulgar life-track, and the light of common day" (ch. 11). In his serene world of art, J. J. is subject neither to the "gusts of passion" nor to the "helpless wandering in the darkness" that torment the other characters whose world is a fallen one (ch. 39). For J. J. his art is a "glorious but harmless war" against reality, a war engaged with palette and brushes as "shield" and "weapons" (ch. 65). As mimic warrior, J. J. exerts no real effect on the world, and his art—like the "castles" of Colonel Newcome—is more wish-fulfilling compensation than interpretation of or alternative to the hard, real world in which Clive and Ethel have to live.

Clive and the Problem of Human Happiness

The handsome Clive Newcome, fair-haired and blue-eyed, enters the novel as "the picture of health, strength, activity and good humour." His laughter and sparkle confirm that he is "just such a youth as has a right to

be the hero of a novel" (ch. 6). Ardent about life, the young Clive plunges
with enthusiasm into the joys it offers an indulged youth and budding
artist. To his "sunny, kindly spirit," life is "welcome": "the day a pleasure;
all Nature a gay feast . . . the night brought him a long sleep, and the
morning a glad waking" (ch. 28). In his innocence he resembles "those
guileless virgins of romance and ballad, who walk smiling through dark
forests charming off dragons and confronting lions; the young man as yet
went through the world harmless; no giant waylaid him as yet" (ch. 28).
The ominous "as yet" signals the precariousness of Clive's youthful im-
munity and looks ahead to the darker world that will transform the "gay
feast" of life into the bitter taste of dust and ashes.

Like the young Arthur Pendennis, Clive is a *Bildungsroman* hero, but
Clive's experience brings him no sustaining moral values like those acknowledged by Pen when he embraced Laura Bell. Where Pen gained a
moral knowledge endowing life with meaning, Clive's knowledge is more
simply existential: he confronts the futilities and pains of human existence
and learns to cope through endurance and resignation. Clive's energy and
joy are eroded by a long, fruitless love, an incompatible marriage, and
"mute battles" with a father who deeply loves but does not understand
him. In a military image expressing the father-son tension Clive indicates
vividly the psychological strains in the Newcome household: "The Colonel
and I are walking on a mine, and that poor little wife of mine is perpetually
flinging little shells to fire it. I sometimes wish it were blown up, and I
were done for" (ch. 66). The death wish only makes explicit the underlying significance of the lassitude and apathy that mark Clive during the
period of his marriage and connection with the Bundelcund bank. In
losing Ethel, Juliet McMaster has argued, Clive loses his will, and the slow
unfolding of the narrative after the loss emphasizes "the protracted pain of
Clive's story, for we see the slow process of his disintegration."[17] Rather
like Clara Pulleyn, who withdrew into brooding silence, Clive sits "silent
and gloomy," the energy of motion and even of language having become
pointless.

Even as his father's bankruptcy rouses him, it heightens the agony of his
existence, for sharp pangs replace the more numbing pain of the days of
prosperity. Clive now "begins the world," scrambling to earn a living from
the precarious trade of artist and suffering a domestic life that is one of the
most harrowing in Victorian fiction. Home is a broken father, a bewildered child, a "coarse female tyrant" who "grudged each morsel which
his father ate," and an "ailing wife" who greets him with "helpless
hysterical cries and reproaches" (ch. 73). Poverty drives Clive to ask his

friend, Pendennis, for money, but his desperation is not merely financial: "I can't stand it at home," he tells Pen. "My heart's almost broken" (ch. 73). Recognition of the "almost broken" heart as the condition of his existence is the knowledge that experience has brought the eager youth who found life "welcome."

The bleakness of this recognition is increased by Clive's perception of himself as trapped in the same cycle of frustration that marked his father's life. The central fact in the lives of both is that each loved one woman and married another. "Your heart was with the other," the married Clive tells the Colonel in a moment of intimacy. "So is mine. It's fatal; it runs in the family, father" (ch. 68). Clive's life repeats that of his father in its pattern of frustrated love, isolation, and, eventually, adoration of the son. The final chapter shows Clive making his young boy his world, endowing him "with his entire wealth of affection" (ch. 80). The plot that in the early part of the narrative looked like the regular, linear plot of the *Bildungsroman*, detailing progress toward maturity, now turns out to be a circular plot illustrating the recurrence of human error and sorrow. *The Newcomes*, Jean Sudrann points out, regards the individual "as simply the agent of his own day in the perpetually retold story of human life."[18] As Sudrann notes, the perspective that all stories are old can provide a comforting distance from immediate event and so lessen the intensity of rage or pain; but it is also fundamentally disquieting, precisely because it robs the moment of any unique significance. "There may be nothing new under and including the sun," Thackeray comments in the Overture, "but it looks fresh every morning." To someone like Clive the knowledge that the freshness inheres only in the innocent perception is demoralizing, generating the sense of futility that shadows his adulthood.

Through its ominous repetitions and parallels (particularly between generations) *The Newcomes* conveys a sense of human life as inevitably flawed. There is something inimical in life itself, the novel implies, something beyond the reach of social reform or goodwill or love itself. "I have been nearly fifty years dying," says Léonore de Florac of her adult life (ch. 47). Gentle spirits like Mme de Florac, W. C. Roscoe wrote in 1856, "shine like glowworms, brightly, but with no influence in the surrounding darkness."[19] Thackeray in fact goes further, dimming their light and denying them any more fulfillment than that experienced by mean souls like Lady Kew. "Between two such women as Madame de Florac and Lady Kew, of course there could be little liking or sympathy," the narrator states but goes on to compare (rather than contrast) the two when he admits: "I don't know that one lady was happier than the other" (ch. 46). Their families fail both; both are alone. Lady Kew takes refuge in incessant movement, from town to ball to castle, but is "for ever uneasy and always alone" (ch. 46). Mme de Florac turns to prayer and to resignation: "One supports the combats of life, but they are long, and one comes from them very wounded" (ch. 53). Life wounds even the shallow Rosey Mackenzie, her placid surface destroyed by poverty, illness, an indifferent husband, and a domineering mother. In a striking moment just before her death Rosey reveals an unexpected depth of suffering when she faces Ethel, who has come to announce the bequest. Gazing at Ethel with a "ghastly smile," Rosey tears her hand away from her mother, leaving behind her wedding ring (ch. 79). Rosey, too, has her darkness and her anguish.[20]

Loss is the keynote of *The Newcomes,* as Thackeray pushes beyond particular social reality to the universal realities of time and death—the ultimate ground of human defeat. Time sours and destroys human lives, its very restorations and compensations, as in the children it brings, turning out to be generally delusive. For Thackeray, time is typically the medium less of growth than of decay. Although he evokes vividly the rare moments when time fulfills rather than denies, emphasis even here tends to fall on transience and hence on loss. Clive and Ethel's happy days at Baden, for instance, are conveyed in part through gay letters written to Colonel Newcome in India, but the narrator interrupts to underline that their joy is long gone. He shatters the fictional illusion of the dramatic present by considering the letters as actual, historical documents, reducing the living voice of Ethel to "faded" writing on yellowed paper, regarding the letters as "mementoes" from the past, "shimmering out of Hades an instant but to sink back again into the cold shades" (ch. 28). In this context Ethel's bantering note becomes ghostly, seems an echo from a tomb.

Underlying the novel is a sense of time as made up of moments informed by no more coherence than that provided by chronology or repetition. The narrative itself—slow and loose—embodies such a sense of time, and Thackeray maintained his leisurely digressive method even in the face of reader impatience with the early sections. "The publishers write and hint that the public has found that the story does not move," Thackeray informed his mother, ". . . but I intend to disregard their petitions" (Letters, 3:346–47). He did, however, incorporate a defense of his method into *The Newcomes* itself, opening Chapter 24 with the statement: "This narrative, as the judicious reader no doubt is aware, is written maturely and at ease, long after the voyage is over whereof it recounts the adventures and perils." Elaborating the metaphor of Clive's life as a sea voyage, the passage absorbs the novel (as an imitation of Clive's life) into the voyage metaphor as well: "In such a history events follow each other without necessarily having a connection with one another. One ship crosses another ship, and, after a visit from one captain to his comrade, they sail away each on his course. The "Clive Newcome" meets a vessel which makes signals that she is short of bread and water; and after supplying her, our captain leaves to see her no more." Within the novel characters drift in and out; minor plots (like that of Clara Pulleyn) connect momentarily with a major plot and then fade out. It is a novel of moments, images, and glimpses, narrative action becoming concentrated only in the final third. Recognizing its richness but disturbed by its untidiness, Henry James delivered the famous judgment that *The Newcomes* (along with *War and Peace* and *The Three Musketeers*) belonged in the category of "large loose baggy monsters."[21]

For all the bleakness of its vision, *The Newcomes* is not a bleak book, and the clue to its oddly affirmative nature lies in a few lines in the epilogue. Here Thackeray enters as himself, commenting on the characters who are rapidly fading away as he (and the reader) return to actuality: "I hardly know whether they are not true: whether they do not live near us somewhere. They were alive, and I heard their voices; but five minutes since was touched by their grief." More than mere whimsy, the sentiments point to the reality Thackeray's characters assumed for him. Striking the keynote of the novel once more, he records a loss. But the sense of loss here is a measure of Thackeray's caring for his creations. Through them he convinces us that human lives do, after all, matter deeply.

Chapter Seven
Replayings: Thackeray's Later Work

Thackeray's later work is a curious mixture of brilliance and banality, often tedious and even disturbing to read. Theoretically interesting, it is less compelling as fiction than his earlier novels, deriving its energy from the critical rather than creative faculty and growing out of a personal and artistic demoralization. Plagued by ill health, Thackeray wearied of life even though he maintained his gregarious habits, acknowledged the benefits of his success, and enjoyed increasingly the company of his daughters. He led an active existence, touring the United States in 1855–56 with lectures on the Hanoverian kings (*The Four Georges,* 1860); running for Parliament in 1857; and editing the successful new *Cornhill Magazine* from 1859 to 1862. But when in 1862 a doctor diagnosed (inaccurately, as it turned out) a fatal illness, Thackeray confessed in a letter: "I wasn't very sorry" (*Letters,* 4:264). His final years were imbued with a premonition of death and with an uneasy conviction that perhaps life was "but a twopenny game after all" ("Autour de Mon Chapeau," *Roundabout Papers*).

Translated into his novels, this state of mind expressed itself in a heightened impatience with and distrust of storytelling. Thackeray would rather have written history than fiction at this stage of his career, and plans for a historical study of the age of Queen Anne were constantly in his mind. But his desire to provide financially for his daughters kept him at his "old trade" of novelist. "I may want to give up novel-writing," he remarked to a friend, "but how refuse when I am paid such prodigious sums?" (*Letters,* 4:136). So he produced two long novels, *The Virginians* (1857–59) and *The Adventures of Philip* (1861–62), as well as the short fiction, *Lovel the Widower* (1860). More congenial was the series of familiar essays for the *Cornhill,* the *Roundabout Papers* (1860–63), but at the time of his sudden death a novel was once more claiming his attention, the unfinished *Denis Duval* (1864).[1]

Thackeray's desire to write history signaled the erosion of his early confidence in the novel as the effective mode for comprehending reality. In contrast to his emphasis at the period of *Vanity Fair* on the realist capacity (and responsibility) of fiction, Thackeray now regarded novels as pleasant but irrelevant trifles. His Roundabout Paper, "On a Lazy Idle Boy," develops the image of novels as "sweets" of which one tires as one matures, while a letter to Anthony Trollope speaks disparagingly of the "tarts" of fiction and stresses that in the *Cornhill* "one of our chief objects . . . is the getting out of novel spinning, and back into the world" (*Letters,* 4:158). Part of the problem was that for Thackeray fiction-making had become too much a mechanical, formulaic activity. "I hate story-making, incidents, surprises, love-making, etc. more and more every day," he commented as he was writing *The Virginians,* and he knew that as a result of this dislike he had "dawdled fatally" in the novel (*Letters,* 4:80, 115).

Reviewers were quick to confirm Thackeray's own criticism. "Of the plot of *The Virginians,*" one of them noted in the *Edinburgh Review,* "we have only to say what the topographer said of the snakes in Iceland. There is none."[2] Remarking that *Philip,* as if in compensation, offers a good deal more plot, Walter Bagehot nevertheless concluded: "as far as 'plot' is concerned *Philip* is a failure."[3] But Thackeray's impatience with plot and with novelistic conventions in general led him to probe more deeply and daringly than ever before the limitations and possibilities of fiction. Always critical and self-aware, Thackeray in his late novels became almost obsessively self-conscious, anticipating in the heightened subjectivity and skepticism of his fiction the direction the modern novel would pursue.

The repetitiousness of Thackeray's late work has tended to obscure its more original implications. The hostile *Saturday Review* accused Thackeray of cynically offering mere "reminiscences of his old novels in profusion,"[4] and Thackeray himself acknowledged that "I have told my tale in the novel department. I can repeat old things in a pleasant way, but I have nothing fresh to say" (*Letters,* 4:242n). Precisely this self-awareness rescues the later narratives from being simply tired re-creations of past efforts. *The Virginians* and *Philip* in particular are replayings in a more profound sense than that of mere repetition: in them Thackeray engages in a reexamination of his own earlier fiction. Appropriately, the novelist who began his career by scrutinizing the conventions of popular novels ends by turning that skepticism on the conventions of his own work.

The Virginians: Revisiting the Esmonds

Growing out of the Preface to *Henry Esmond* where Esmond's daughter, Rachel Warrington, referred to the "fatal differences" that separated her sons in the American Revolutionary War, *The Virginians* focuses on her twins, George and Harry Warrington, but begins their story twenty years before the conflict alluded to in Rachel's Preface. In 1756 Esmond's grandson, nineteen-year-old Harry Warrington, arrives in England. The younger of the twins, Harry is in mourning for his brother, George, believed killed in a skirmish between the French and English in the American colonies a year ago. The lives of the brothers have been dominated by their mother, an early widow whose deepest affection has always been reserved for her own father. Appropriately, she is known in Virginia as Madam Esmond, rather than Warrington, and she emerges as a snobbish, pious, and irrational woman who "never came near man or woman, but she tried to domineer over them" (ch. 4). Her relationship with her sons is uneasy, and Harry escapes with relief his oppressive home.

Once in England, he eagerly seeks out his English relatives, Lord Castlewood and his family, only to be met with indifference until he is taken up by Baroness Bernstein, the wealthy aunt of both Harry and Lord Castlewood. Her presence introduces vivid memories of *Henry Esmond,* for Baroness Bernstein is the once-enchanting Beatrix Esmond, now old and fat, her loneliness assuaged by card games and by manipulation of her greedy relations. Witty and corrupt, Beatrix Bernstein epitomizes the sophisticated decadence of the Old World to which Harry, the New World innocent, is now exposed.[5] His Castlewood cousins turn out to be cheats, liars, and gamblers, their society motivated by greed, selfishness, and falseness.

The impressionable and naive Harry is quickly seduced into a promise of marriage by his scheming cousin, Maria Castlewood, a woman old enough to be his mother.[6] He also falls victim to the hollow glitter of the fashionable world, taking up gambling and generally indulging himself in the idle, vain existence of a young aristocrat. But he retains his sense of honor, maintaining his pledge to Maria, despite his own increasing repulsion to her and despite the powerful pressure exerted by Aunt Beatrix to break the engagement. And he responds positively to the Lambert family, whose firm moral values and harmonious pastoral life underline the corruption of the Castlewoods and their circle. The lively and intelligent Hetty Lambert falls in love with Harry but masks her passion, and Harry (characteristically) fails to penetrate her disguise. He is equally obtuse in reading the character of his paternal relatives, Sir Miles Warrington and his family, a pretentious and hypocritical set affecting a generosity and concern whose falseness is exposed when they refuse to help their nephew after a wild gambling streak leaves him in prison, penniless and in debt.

At this critical juncture the lost brother, George, makes a dramatic entrance to rescue Harry. With the appearance of George (he had been imprisoned by the French and bribed his way out), Harry's status alters radically from that of heir to dependent younger brother, and Maria ends the engagement. Harry joins the army and moves into the background of the novel. In the second half of *The Virginians* the center of concern is George whose melancholy and introverted nature recalls his grandfather Esmond. In Chapter 72 George suddenly assumes narration of the novel which now (like *Henry Esmond*) takes the form of personal memoirs written for his descendants.

Unwilling to return to Virginia, George stays in London where he studies law in a casual fashion, writes a moderately successful play, and falls in love with Hetty's older sister, Theo. Unlike his brother, George is not tempted by the fashonable world; he moves in more intellectual and literary circles (Samuel Johnson is a good friend), and his moral values, notably the domestic values so central to the Victorian novel, remain firm. All goes smoothly until George's mother insults Theo's father, General Lambert, by implying that the Lambert parents have schemed to marry Theo to her son. His honor stung, General Lambert orders the separation of the lovers. But after witnessing their anguish, he relents, and George and Theo marry. Poverty soon threatens the young couple as George's funds run out and his second play fails. A fortunate inheritance (including a title and country estate) relieves the situation, assuring their future material comfort.

The quarrel between England and her American colonies now begins to assume significance. In Virginia Harry has married Fanny Mountain, a domineering woman who has inspired him with her own zeal for American independence. Since he is in England, George adopts the English side of the question, but his complex mind allows no simple apportioning of right and wrong. He stresses his moral uncertainty, declaring that he does not know "which side was in the right, or whether both were not?" (ch. 84). Despite their political difference, the brothers remain friends; but during the Revolutionary War George and Harry command regiments on the opposing sides. Here Thackeray avoids showing direct confrontation, allowing George to learn only after a battle, for example, that Harry was fighting against him in the same engagement. As a result of such knowledge, George decides finally to withdraw from this "fratricidal contest" to which he is not really committed.

He returns to England to his peaceful domestic existence, while Harry (whose shrewish Fanny has died to the relief of all) marries again more happily and stays in Virginia where old Madam Esmond lives on. The narrative concludes with an image of George invoking the reassuring family circle as he shuts the book he has just finished writing and goes to bed, "with a blessing on those now around me asleep."

The novel as reinterpretation. *The Virginians* rewrites *Henry Esmond,* using the earlier text as constant reference in order to reveal that Esmond's descendants play out "a jaded and pointless parody."[7] So the Jacobite cause for which Henry Esmond risked his life becomes mere sentimental allegiance in his daughter and young grandsons, an affectation in the context of Virginia. Repeated plot details, like the search for hidden documents that figures near the end of both novels, are similarly emptied of significance. Whereas in *Henry Esmond* the documents proving Esmond's claim to the title were central to both action and theme, in *The Virginians* the documents proving the Warrington claim to the Virginia estate function only in a subplot of peripheral interest. The gestures of *Henry Esmond* survive, but the informing substance and existential urgency are missing. For Harry (who re-creates Frank Castlewood) and George (who re-creates Esmond) the scope for action has narrowed, and the attenuation of the connection between private and public history has reduced the tensions and the stakes.

Relationships lose their resonance; the emotional texture of the world has thinned. The oedipal content of George's ambivalent response to his mother may recall one of the strains in Henry Esmond's response to Rachel, but *The Virginians* simplifies the oedipal motif and dissipates its tensions early in a deliberate, comic replaying of a crucial confrontation in *Henry Esmond.* Eliminating the complication of Rachel's adulterous passion for Esmond, *The Virginians* concentrates on its incestuous component in the episode involving George Warrington, his mother (Rachel), and the supposed suitor, George Washington. When the jealous son challenges the innocent Washington to a duel, he models his behavior on Lord Castlewood's challenge to the earlier Rachel's would-be seducer, Lord Mohun, in *Henry Esmond*: "Do you not remember, in our grandfather's life of himself," George asks Harry, "how he says that Lord Castlewood fought Lord Mohun on a pretext of a quarrel at cards? and never so much as hinted at the lady's name, who was the real cause of the duel? I took my hint, I confess, from *that,* Harry" (ch. 11). But where Castlewood's challenge ended in his death and in Esmond's bitter estrangement from Rachel, George's attempt to re-create Esmond's text ends in farce. He has entirely misinterpreted the case, and the novel treats his melodramatic response with amused irony. At the last moment the duel is aborted by Mrs. Mountain (Madam Esmond's companion) who leaps on a horse to gallop up and clarify matters. In contrast to *Henry Esmond* this dramatization of sexual rivalry leads nowhere, has no significant effect on characters or action, and stands primarily to point the reduction of passion and tension and act in *The Virginians*.

Listening to Harry's account of the episode, Beatrix Bernstein—her decayed presence itself a reminder of the divergence between the two worlds—recognizes in his "simple tales about his mother traits of family resemblance" (ch. 14). She goes on to imply that Madam Esmond's insistence that Washington is simply a friend rings false. We recall that in *Henry Esmond* Beatrix intuited early the nature of her own mother's feeling for Esmond, but once again what was a crucial insight in *Henry Esmond* proves to be a minor sidelight in *The Virginians* where Madam Esmond's response to Washington is of little importance. Furthermore, Madam Esmond herself is a sardonic version of her mother, exhibiting Rachel's self-deception, jealousy, and possessiveness but lacking her warmth, emotional depth, and self-control. Like Beatrix Bernstein (and all the later Castlewoods, for that matter), she stands as testament to the debasement that time has wrought in the Esmond family. Significantly, Harry tells Beatrix his story under the portraits of the Esmonds featured in the earlier novel (a visual emblem of the dependence of the two texts), and he fails to recognize in the old woman the original of the beautiful girl in the portrait before him. The moment invokes not only the expected commonplaces about the transience of beauty but also the gap between the world of the two novels. Although *Henry Esmond* is a constant presence in *The Virginians*, it is a presence experienced paradoxically as an absence. As Jack P. Rawlins points out, the memory of *Henry Esmond* generates a recognition in the reader of what is lost in *The Virginians*, so defining the world of the later novel as even worse than pointless: "it is meaningless *where once there was meaning*."[8]

But *The Virginians* pushes its skepticism even further: it places in question even this assumption that a meaningful world once existed by scrutinizing the text supporting that assumption. While the replay of *Henry Esmond* reveals the triviality and irrelevance of actions in the decayed Warrington world, it inevitably implicates action in *Henry Esmond* as well. The latter-day world of *The Virginians* may indeed represent a falling off from the richer possibilities of the world of *Henry Esmond,* but do Esmond's own recollection and interpretation of that world stand up? Is there perhaps something suspect in the very order he made out of the actions of his own life? Building on the potentially subversive perspective introduced into *Henry Esmond* itself in the Preface and footnotes (see Chapter 5), *The Virginians* reinterprets Esmond's narrative with its affirmation of a self fulfilled through time and completed by the love of Rachel. Thackeray not only rewrites but rereads *Henry Esmond* in a sophisticated narrative strategy that sets the two texts in play against each other.

Where Esmond ended his narrative with an image of life in Virginia as a "happy and serene" Indian summer, *The Virginians* undercuts the idyllic picture. Esmond, we are now told, "submitted to life, rather than enjoyed it," having suffered "some bankruptcy of his heart" from which he never recovered. Accordingly, he "never was in better spirits than in his last hours when he was going to lay [life] down" (ch. 3). His glowing image of Rachel is also subject to reinterpretation, not simply through her reincarnation in her namesake but through direct commentary by her other daughter, Beatrix, who describes to George the oppressiveness of living with an "angel": "My poor mother was so perfect that she never could forgive me for being otherwise. Ah, mon Dieu! how she used to oppress me with those angelical airs!" (ch. 54). Thinking of "his own melancholy youth" under another pious Rachel, George agrees silently. More poignantly, the dying old Beatrix declares that her mother "does not love me. She never did. Why don't you, mother?" (ch. 83). The worldly Beatrix, of course, is no final authority. Thackeray has set in motion her interpretation beside that of Esmond in order to generate questions rather than point conclusions. This is his method throughout, as in his allowing the dubious Beatrix and the equally dubious Madam Esmond to stand as the two voices most insistent on Esmond's heroic stature.

Thackeray's placing in doubt his own earlier text is but part of more general skeptical and reductive processes in *The Virginians,* a novel remarkable for its dismissal of values and forms central to Victorian fiction. Changing heroes midway, suddenly switching narrators, Thackeray unsettles assumptions about focus and continuity. And a new note of contempt enters the fiction, most notably in his treatment of first love. While Thackeray has always exposed the delusions of romance and the follies of adolescence, he now demonstrates a bitterness and impatience absent from the more tolerant and genial evocation of youthful delusions in early novels like *Pendennis.* In *The Virginians* Harry's infatuation with the aging Maria prompts a savage demystification. The rose Harry treasures as a gift from Maria is derided as "a bunch of amputated and now decomposing greens," while the lady herself is imaged as one of the "stale, old, leering witches" preying on unsuspecting males (ch. 18). Hand holding is dismissed with the reductive question: "What good can there be in pulling and pressing a thumb and four fingers?" (ch. 20). Although the deep and tender love of George and Theo is spared such contempt, Thackeray's dark vision infects even the domestic ideal. Late in the novel George admits: "There came a period of my life, when having reached the summit of felicity I was quite tired of the prospect I had there: I yawned in Eden, and said, 'Is this all?' " (ch. 85). Assuming a playful tone, he promises to make his "confessions," but instead the editor intervenes to record that three pages have been torn out of the manuscript.

This curious hiatus has the effect of a void opening up suddenly and closing, and George continues his narration evenly. While we should not make too much of the odd gap, the general tone of George's narration reinforces the sense that despite his genuine and lasting love for his wife and family, he has spent a large part of his life in melancholy and boredom for which there is no relief. For self-conscious and skeptical spirits like George, the novel suggests, there is no answer, no possibility of profound fulfillment in life. From this perspective the novel's notoriously loose plot takes on a deeper significance, revealing more than Thackeray's weariness with fiction or rejection of popular literary convention. Robert L. Caserio has suggested that "when writers and readers of novels lose interest in plot and story, they appear to lose faith in the meaning and moral value of acts."[9] *The Virginians* implies such a loss of faith: Thackeray here gives up on plot because he gives up on the possibility of meaningful action.

The Adventures of Philip: Thackeray's Last *Bildungsroman*

Like *The Virginians, The Adventures of Philip* revisits Thackeray's earlier works, resurrecting characters from *The Newcomes* and *Pendennis,* but for the germ of *Philip* Thackeray went back twenty years to "A Shabby Genteel Story" written for *Fraser's Magazine* in 1840. Here he had offered an unfinished, anti-Cinderella story, recounting the tale of Caroline Gann, a lower-class heroine abused by a stepmother and stepsisters, who falls in love with an upper-class rogue calling himself George Brandon and naively elopes with him. *Philip* takes up the narrative many years later when Caroline, deserted by Brandon after a brief, false marriage, has established herself as a nurse and boarding-house keeper, her nursing skill having

earned her the affectionate epithet, "Little Sister." Brandon has become
Dr. Firmin, a fashionable society doctor, whose valid marriage to an earl's
niece (now dead) has produced the Philip of the title.

But more significant than the relationship between the early short story
and the novel is the relationship between *Philip* and *Pendennis,* Thackeray's
first *Bildungsroman.* Like the young Arthur Pendennis, Philip Firmin is an
autobiographical hero, his bohemian tastes, loss of fortune, difficult
courtship, and journalistic struggles being modeled on Thackeray's own.
Like Pen, Philip has a single, difficult parent, loves the wrong woman
before loving the right one, and encounters financial difficulties and
setbacks in life before the novel resolves his problems. But Philip's
extroverted nature and simple-mindedness distinguish him from the more
thoughtful and complex Pen who reappears as the narrator of *Philip* and
functions as the alter ego of the older Thackeray.[10] When the young hero
of *Pendennis* turns up as the older narrator of *Philip,* telling a story similar
to the one in which he figured years before, his presence inevitably
juxtaposes the two texts, setting up a complicated reverberation between
them.

Both novels turn to a biblical parable for their structure—*Pendennis* to
the Prodigal Son and *Philip* to the Good Samaritan—but the choice of
parable signals an important difference in the function of hero and plot in
the two novels. Where the Prodigal Son focuses attention on the hero as
the subject of scrutiny and identifies him as a morally flawed being whom
experience (plot) puts to the test, the Good Samaritan shifts attention from
the central figure (the robbed man) to concentrate on the conduct of others
in relation to him. The robbed man serves as a touchstone by which to
measure the charity and responsibility of the passersby. In *Pendennis* plot
tests the hero; in *Philip* it tests those around him, as the full title of the
novel makes clear: *The Adventures of Philip on His Way Through the World,
Shewing Who Robbed Him, Who Helped Him and Who Passed Him By.*

In the parable the character of the robbed man is irrelevant, as turns out
to be the case with Philip Firmin, Thackeray's most obnoxious hero. All
through the novel Thackeray teases the reader with his awareness of
Philip's mediocrity and moral flaws ("Mr. Phil's views of life were not very
exalted, were they?") and threatens playfully to depose him as hero but in
the end rewards him gleefully. While the moral implications of *Philip*'s
version of the Good Samaritan may not be biblical,[11] the biblical reference
helps to explain the configurations of the novel, including the odd fact that
Thackeray's most boisterous and aggressive hero remains passive at critical
junctures of his career. As the robbed man, Philip must allow others to

display their moral fiber by acting or not acting, but the passive function sits uneasily in this active character, and the resulting strain explodes into the violence of Philip's frequent quarrels.[12]

The story opens with Philip in an aggressive enough posture: he deliberately humiliates his father by walking out in the middle of a speech that Dr. Firmin is delivering at the public school they both attended. The moment is symptomatic in a novel where, as Robert Colby notes, the "filial devotion central to all Thackeray's domestic novels . . . has turned to gall."[13] Exactly what has turned the father-son relationship into gall is never entirely clear, but Philip's deep resentment of his parent has something to do with his father's treatment of his mother and something to do with Philip's suspicions about his treatment of Caroline Gann. Caroline, who has adopted the false name of her seducer and calls herself Mrs. Brandon, entered Philip's life as a nurse in his childhood and now functions as a surrogate mother. In her presence Philip is tender and respectful, but with his father he is defiant and rude.

Somehow Philip's naturally frank and hearty nature has been "poisoned," and he is extravagant, reckless, and unruly. He mixes with a low bohemian crowd, to the consternation of his snobbish father, and he is expelled from university for rebellious pranks. Repelled by Firmin's social ambitions and concern with respectable appearance, Philip adopts a manner directly opposed to that of his father: "[Firmin] was so grave, so polite, so complimentary, so artificial, that Phil, in revolt at such hypocrisy, chose to be frank, cynical, and familiar" (ch. 5). Cushioned by the income from an inheritance of £30,000 from his mother, Philip can afford to indulge his rebellious instincts and to lead an idle life, supposedly studying law but more assiduously studying taverns.

Despite his preference for the non-genteel, Philip is in love with a highly genteel woman, his cousin, Agnes Twysden. The ambitious Twysdens are a mean lot, scraping and toadying their way through the world, and Agnes is a true Twysden. Calculating and frigid, she plays with Philip, enticing him but avoiding commitment lest a better prospect appear. Philip's pursuit of Agnes, however, lacks any real urgency, and Pen is quick to reassure the reader that his hero suffers "only a little brief delusion of the senses" from which he will recover in a few chapters (ch. 9).

At twenty-two Philip finds his affairs at a stalemate: he and Agnes remain at the same point; the tension between father and son continues; Philip himself drifts in idleness. The catalyst for change takes the shape of a dingy and drunken clergyman, Tufton Hunt, who had conducted the false marriage between Firmin and Caroline. Made confident by his knowledge of many uncomfortable truths about Firmin's past, Hunt moves into the Firmin house and obtains money from the doctor. But when he tries overt blackmail over the story of Caroline, Firmin outflanks him by confessing the story to Philip, who is impressed and softened by his father's frankness. The thwarted Hunt then enlists the Twysdens in a complicated plot to have Philip declared illegitimate, but a self-sacrificing lie by Caroline Brandon destroys their scheme.

Ironically, the removal of this threat turns out to be a hollow victory, only a prelude to the collapse of the whole edifice of Philip's life. He loses Agnes and (more significant) his fortune. One night Dr. Firmin sneaks out of England, having speculated away not only his own money but also the inheritance in trust for Philip. The son is left with £200, but (rather like the young Thackeray in a similar situation) Philip is more relieved than sorry, for he has long anticipated a "smash" as he tells Pen: "Without understanding why or wherefore, I have always been looking out for this" (ch. 15).

With the departure of Dr. Firmin and Philip's loss of fortune, the Samaritan theme announced in the title becomes a more insistent presence in the novel. Robbed by his own father, Philip soon learns that relatives (like the Twysdens and his rich great-uncle, Lord Ringwood) pass him by, while friends outside the family (like Caroline Brandon and the Pendennis family) come to his aid. In an effort to earn money Philip turns to literary journalism (for which his talent is slight), but his energies are very shortly devoted primarily to love when he meets Charlotte Baynes, sweet and rather simple-minded daughter of General Baynes, Philip's trustee and legally liable for the fraud against the estate he was charged with protecting. Philip, in fact, meets the Baynes family in Boulogne where they have fled to avoid their responsibility to Philip and where it becomes apparent quickly that the family is ruled by the formidable Mrs. Baynes, another of Thackeray's possessive and domineering mothers, whose emotional fierceness and ambition bode ill for the future of Charlotte and Philip.

Mrs. Baynes remains quiescent until Philip insults Lord Ringwood and ruins his chances of a handsome legacy; then she begins to exert relentless pressure on Charlotte to break her engagement to Philip: "A yellow old woman . . . would come, night after night, to the side of her little bed; and there stand, and with her grim voice bark against Philip" (ch. 23). Like Philip's father (whose house contained a portrait of Abraham sacrificing Isaac), Charlotte's mother turns out to be a monstrous parent, her daughter likened to Iphigenia, the Greek heroine sacrificed by her father. When Philip's temper flares against yet another relative, his egregious cousin, Ringwood Twysden (whom he tosses into a fountain during a society ball), Mrs. Baynes succeeds in browbeating Charlotte's father into declaring the engagement null. Charlotte is kept apart from Philip but refuses to deny her love for him, the strain of her position bringing her to the verge of nervous collapse. Ashamed of his conduct, General Baynes turns against his wife and, before he dies, he blesses the young couple.

Spurred by Caroline Brandon, Philip's friends arrange an editorial post for him on the *Pall Mall Gazette.* He and Charlotte marry, living with Caroline of whose love for Philip Charlotte becomes increasingly jealous. Domestic problems mount when Philip quarrels with his employer, Mugford, a friendly, self-made man whose vulgarity grates on the more gently bred Philip. Having lost his job with Mugford, Philip is once again rescued by friends who find him another position. But Philip's efforts at achieving financial security for his growing family are undermined by the demands of his father. Dr. Firmin has settled in New York where he has gained sympathy by spreading rumors that his son ruined him, but he keeps drawing on the impoverished Philip. Matters come to a head when he forges his son's signature to a large promissory note that is now in the possession of the disreputable Tufton Hunt in England. Philip decides reluctantly that filial duty compels him to honor the note, but the more tough-minded Caroline Brandon disagrees. Luring Hunt into her house, she chloroforms him, then steals and burns the bill.

Despite this relief, Philip's situation worsens. The family has moved out of Caroline's house, and it soon becomes clear that Charlotte is a poor household manager. At the same time, Philip's temper (directed this time at another cousin, Philip Ringwood) costs him his job once more. In dire straits, he appeals to his mother-in-law to pay him money she owes; she refuses and Philip wonders bitterly "whether the thieves who attacked the man in the parable were robbers of his own family" (ch. 41). Philip's fortunes reach their lowest point when Charlotte falls into a fever after giving birth to a third child, and he must cope "with a wife in extremity, with crying infants, with hunger menacing at the door" (ch. 41). At this crisis, the rejected and vulgar Mugfords, informed by Caroline of the family's distress, arrive with baskets of food and the offer of a job. The rescue is completed by the discovery in the novel's last chapter of the lost will of Lord Ringwood that leaves Philip a legacy ensuring his financial security for life.

In its conclusion the novel circles back to Dr. Firmin and Caroline Brandon, the characters who originally inspired the story. Firmin remarries in the United States only to succumb to yellow fever three months later. Oddly affected by his remarriage, Caroline is even more strangely disturbed by his death, putting on mourning and having herself announced as "Mrs. Firmin." She herself dies eventually of a fever caught from a patient but (like Helen Pendennis in *Pendennis*) remains a presence in Philip's family where all, including the once-jealous Charlotte, speak fondly of her "as though she were among them still."

Philip and narrative convention. In *Philip*, as in *The Virginians*, external act becomes less capable of signifying meaning, and plot is devalued accordingly.[14] Throughout the novel Pen consistently undermines his plot, declaring that "I do not seek to create even surprises in this modest history" (ch. 8) and destroying narrative suspense by revealing outcome, as when he announces beforehand how the relationships with Agnes and with Charlotte will turn out. Moreover, he draws ostentatious attention to the artificiality of his own contrivances, airily instructing readers in an important confrontation scene to "place" characters "in what posture you will" (ch. 27); chuckling over the convenience of the lost will; and bragging that "love-making" is "the very easiest part of the novel-writer's business" because the writer "who knows his business may be thinking about anything else" (ch. 23).

Pen's attitude to his narrative reflects Thackeray's heightened awareness of the difficulty of penetrating to the truth of things and his increased skepticism about the adequacy of conventional plot to discover or express what matters. While such skepticism leads to the evasive flippancy of *Philip*, it also generates significant experiments with fictional form, as in Thackeray's radical departure from chronological narrative in the opening chapters of the novel. Joseph P. Baker sees in *Philip* "the *least* direct narrative of any novel before the twentieth century" and nowhere is this indirection more striking than in the way Thackeray introduces his story.[15] He opens the novel with a childhood illness of Philip at an unspecified time prior to the dramatic present, then drops this subject to leap ahead to a Philip of college age, leaving unexplained the initial focus on the illness whose purpose begins to become apparent only at the end of Chapter 3. Darting backwards and forwards in the history of Philip and Pendennis, the opening chapters juggle time periods so rapidly and abruptly that a first reading produces bewilderment. Chapter 1, for example, shifts among four distinct time periods and Chapter 2 among at least seven. Leaving vague exact times and locations, Pen disrupts sequence to provide glimpses of Philip (and himself) now as schoolboy, now as middle-aged man, now as adolescent.

"I take up the biography here and there," Pen explains, "so as to give the best idea I may of my friend's character" (ch. 6). The emphasis is not on story (with its clear temporal flow) but on the atemporal "idea" or interpretation. The discontinuous technique combines with Pen's hints, guesses, and questions ("In the midst of what dark family mystery was I?") to imply the difficulty of interpreting the opaque world in which the Firmins live, a world of hidden meanings and deceptive surfaces. "Have you made up your mind on the question of seeming and being in the world?" Pen asks in Chapter 4 as he prepares to introduce the Twysdens, obvious examples of a disjunction between "seeming" and "being" as they cover the reality of poverty and meanness with the appearance of wealth and generosity. But not all disjunctions are so superficial or so clear and deliberate, and to probe the deeper strata of civilized existence the externalizations of ordinary plot are inadequate.

In *Philip,* Juliet McMaster remarks, the literal narrative is often banal and languid but its metaphoric substructure presents a dark and violent world. Images of murder, cannibalism, and execution permeate the text, suggesting that "under the polite forms and energetically maintained surfaces, husbands and wives torment each other, parents victimise their children, and people lay traps and pounce on victims."[16] This sinister view of personal (especially familial) relations and the sense of potentially explosive tension between surface and depth control the presentation of the Firmin household with its mysterious and profound tension between father and son. The Firmin house itself is emblematic, its exterior "as handsome as might be" but its interior silent, dark, and full of funereal ornaments. When Pen asks, "What skeleton was there in the closet?", the proverbial phrase assumes a chilling resonance in light of the actual skeletons to be found in the abandoned lecture room in the doctor's house.

It is a house of secrets and of secret unhappiness. Philip remembers his parents when he was a child: "how silent they were when together, and how terrified she always seemed before him" (ch. 7). His own relationship with his father is marked by deception and victimization, and Firmin evolves into a parasite feeding off his son's slender earnings. Invoking Abraham's sacrifice of Isaac as well as the irony of his father's profession of doctor, Philip comments bitterly: "He does not sacrifice me at one operation; but there will be a final one some day, and I shall bleed no more" (ch. 37). Similarly violent imagery defines Philip's youthful intuition of threatening disaster: "I always feel as if a little sword was dangling over my skull which will fall some day and split it" (ch. 7).

That vain, ambitious, and self-dramatizing egotist, Dr. Firmin, embodies most memorably the mysterious nature of the world of *Philip*. His characterization hints at dark recesses, tangled labyrinths, and a kind of tormented self-knowledge. Once he flees to New York, Firmin dwindles into a rather flat villain, but before his departure Thackeray endows him with a powerful and intriguing life that eludes ready categorization. With his "very white false teeth," "black whiskers," "glaring eyes," and "fierce black eyebrows," Firmin fits the pattern of melodramatic villain, but Thackeray immediately deepens the characterization by allowing Firmin some complexity of response. In Chapter 1 he and Philip glare at one another: "Wicked rage and hate seemed to flash from the doctor's eyes, and anon came a look of wild pitiful supplication towards the guest [Pendennis], which was most painful to bear." Offsetting Firmin's "stereotyped smile" are the "sad" dark eyes that seem to look out "into a great blank desert" (ch. 3). Thackeray hints at an inner void and despair, for Firmin knows that "his boy's heart has revolted from him" and he "lies awake in the night-watches and thinks how he is alone" (ch. 10). But as public man Firmin is a skilled actor who knows how to deliver "a neat speech from behind his ruffled shirt," how to use gesture affectingly, and how to stage-manage his entrances and exits, including his final exit from England when he lulls suspicion by convincingly receiving a fake telegram summoning him to the bedside of a noble patient in Germany. Even through the public role Thackeray continues to convey a sense of inner life, of unspoken knowledge, and of complicated relationships underlying Firmin's smooth surface. Recalling another occasion when the doctor relied on the false summons trick, for example, Pen states: "I think Phil's father knew we knew he was acting. However, he went through the comedy quite gravely" (ch. 7).

Through his handling of plot and character in *Philip* Thackeray suggests that the reality he seeks is elusive, obscure; through his handling of the narrator he confronts more directly the problem of interpretation. In Victorian fiction the narrator is typically the valid interpreter of the story and the authority for the interpretation. To support his privileged position, the narrator functions as communal mind, participating in and articulating the general consciousness of the predominantly middle-class culture of Victorian society.[17] Drawing on that culture and adopting an impersonal, usually formal tone that inspires trust, the narrator conveys an authority and perspective for interpretation transcending the limited, subjective viewpoint of the individual. Thackeray was always suspicious of this authoritative stance; accordingly, his narrators have always been more personal and slippery than those of writers like George Eliot or Trollope. But in *Philip* the characteristic Thackerayan emphasis on the fallibility of the narrator becomes an almost obsessive tearing down of narrative authority when Thackeray foregrounds the personal and insecure voice of Arthur Pendennis.

Adopting informal and colloquial rhythms, Pen continually draws attention to the dependence of the entire narrative on his perspective, his language, his inferences. As early as Chapter 3 he stresses the speculative nature of his activity when he admits: "The story came to me piecemeal; from confessions here, admissions there, deductions of my own." He continues: "I could not, of course, be present at many of the scenes which I shall have to relate as though I had witnessed them; and the posture, language, and inward thoughts of Philip and his friends, as here related, no doubt are fancies of the narrator in many cases." Despite subjective interpolations, Pen claims, his story is "as authentic as many histories," an ironic assertion given the tendency of Thackeray's novels (including this one) to undercut the authenticity of actual histories. Shifting ground, Pen introduces next the standard of "verisimilitude," advising the reader to give the story "only . . . such an amount of credence as he may judge that its verisimilitude warrants" (ch. 3). But the realist appeal to verisimilitude sits oddly in a novel whose narrator persists in pointing out how much wish-fulfillment or reader response determine the shape of his story, as when Pen reassures us that Philip and Agnes will not marry because "I am not such a savage towards my readers or hero, as to make them undergo the misery of such a marriage" (ch. 9). The general effect of such narrative self-consciousness is to make clear that a novel is a made thing and made by someone. Thackeray insists on exposing the pretense on which much realist fiction depends: that the novel is a mirror on the world, reflecting it directly with the narrator functioning more as impersonal medium than individual consciousness.[18]

Pen in *Philip* is very much an individual and a nervous, self-mocking, and equivocal individual at that, continually undermining himself as narrator. "What is this?" he asks at one point. "I profess to be an impartial chronicler of poor Phil's fortunes, misfortunes, friendships, and what-nots, and am getting almost as angry with these Twysdens as Philip ever was himself" (ch. 9). He will hint at personal (often malicious) motives behind certain of his characterizations. After exposing "these Twysdens" earlier in the book, wriggling and twisting and pushing their way forward, Pen stops: "What is this? Am I angry because Twysden has left off asking me to his vinegar and chopped hay?" (ch. 4). The dreadful Mrs.

Baynes offers another instance. Discovering that she considers Pen and his wife to be snobs, Pen asserts that "if Mrs. General Baynes thought some people were 'stuck-up people,' some people can—and hereby do by these presents—pay off Mrs. Baynes, by furnishing the public with a candid opinion of that lady's morals, manners, and character" (ch. 20). Playful as they may be, such strategies shatter conventional narrative distance, so crucial to creating the sense of a reliable, objective interpretation. This is not to suggest that Pen is unreliable but to stress the extent to which Thackeray works to keep the reader aware of the personal, and therefore limited, perspective disguised by the authoritative narrative voice common to Victorian novels.

To Thackeray all knowledge is partial, uncertain; all interpretations only possibilities. Toward the end of *Philip* Pen muses about the fact that some of his characters have appeared in a negative light and remarks that "perhaps, if a biography could be written from their point of view, some other novelist might show how Philip and *his* biographer were a pair of selfish worldlings unworthy of credit" (ch. 41). Such moments draw attention to interpretation as problematic and alert us to how much our reading and understanding of novels depends on the assumption of a particular perspective. By bringing to the surface of his fiction the assumptions and artificialities involved in the working of plot, character, and narrator, Thackeray demonstrates that what so often seems transparent or natural in a literary work is really opaque or conventional. His is a sophisticated insight into narrative, and at its sharpest in the late novels which stand less as fictions than as explorations of the fictional process.

Roundabout Papers, Lovel the Widower and *Denis Duval*

Upon completing *Philip,* Thackeray wrote "De Finibus," a Roundabout Paper about ending—ending novels and ending life: "Another Finis written. Another mile-stone passed on this journey from birth to the next world!" As he moves in this essay from fiction to life and back again—thinking about his characters, about the working of his own imagination, about the personal history behind the words he has written—Thackeray strikes the meditative keynote of the *Roundabout Papers*. These papers for the *Cornhill* are personal meditations in the mode of the familiar essay, casual and associative in structure, often inspired by a trivial observation, but no less serious for their deliberate understatement of their own seriousness. Invoking the example of Michel de Montaigne, whose famous seventeenth-century *Essays* established the personal essay, Thackeray claims the right to "wander who knows whither" and to make himself the subject of his literary conversation: "That right line 'I' is the very shortest, simplest, straightforwardest means of communication between us, and stands for what it is worth and no more" ("On Two Children in Black"). In his "essaykins," as Thackeray calls them in "On a Hundred Years Hence," he is coming to terms with himself, with the passage of time and the prospect of death: "Yet a few chapters more, and then the last: after which, behold Finis itself come to an end, and the Infinite begun" ("De Finibus").

The Roundabouts touch on a variety of topics: the American Civil War ("On Half a Loaf"); the thin veneer of respectability ("Ogres"); the vogue of spiritualism ("The Notch on the Axe"); a London murder ("On Two Roundabout Papers Which I Intended to Write"); the problems of being an editor ("Thorns in the Cushion"). But time is their dominant theme and Thackeray consciously presents himself as a man whose time is running out. "As we go on the down-hill journey," he writes, "the mile-stones are grave-stones, and on each more and more names are written" ("On Letts's Diary"). Such awareness brings no self-pity or bitterness in the Roundabouts, only a rich suspension of urgency which allows Thackeray to muse over his days and ways. Unlike the ancient woman without memory in one of his most powerful pieces, "On Some Carp in Sans Souci," Thackeray remembers, finding comfort in remembering and in recording what he remembers.[19] His stance is deliberately (even defiantly) retrospective, summed up in his image of himself in Time's speeding chariot sitting "with his back to the horses, and his face to the past" ("On A Joke I Once Heard From the Late Thomas Hood"). In this posture Thackeray provides vivid glimpses of his childhood and youth ("Tunbridge Toys," "De Juventute"), the recollections extending beyond personal memory to become part of the memory of a generation, the generation that knew England before railways forever changed its landscape and the speed of life. "We who have lived before railways were made," he says in "De Juventute," "belong to another world." Facetiously, he bemoans the appalling decline in the beauty of ballet dancers; less facetiously, he lovingly celebrates the novels on which his generation grew up, especially the stories of Walter Scott and Alexander Dumas ("On a Lazy Idle Boy," "On a Peal of Bells").

The *Roundabout Papers* were bracketed by two short fictions in the *Cornhill: Lovel the Widower,* which appeared at the beginning of the series, and the unfinished *Denis Duval,* published after the Roundabouts had concluded. Both stories feature the personalized narrative perspective characteristic of Thackeray's later work, but the contrast between the two is extraordinary. *Lovel* is a strange, brilliant but disturbing work, its inward-turning and skeptical narrative linking it to *The Virginians* and *Philip*. Ostensibly another version of the Cinderella story, the novel is narrated by Charles Batchelor, friend of the titular hero, Fred Lovel. Batchelor sets out to relate the social success of Bessy Prior, daughter of a drunken father and shabby genteel mother, who rises from dancer to governess to wife of the wealthy Lovel. But it is less Bessy and Lovel's story than Batchelor's own problems of self-definition that dominate the novel and determine its structure.[20]

External events recede to highlight internal events: the inner plot of Batchelor's frustrated intentions and emotional failure. Courting Bessy and failing to win her, Batchelor repeats the pattern of an earlier, unsuccessful courtship of another woman and exposes his profound insecurity. Although the story is simple, the narration is not. Batchelor's "I" turns out to be far from the straightforward means of communication that Thackeray claims for this pronoun in "On Two Children in Black." Witness a minor moment in the narrative when Batchelor addresses the reader to explain his abandonment of chronological development at the introduction of Bessy Prior: "You see, as I beheld her, a heap of memories struck upon me, and I could not help chattering; when of course—and you are perfectly right, only you might just as well have left the observation alone: for I knew quite well what you were going to say—when I had much better have held my tongue" (ch. 2). Uneasy as both narrator and lover, Batchelor cannot tell a straightforward story, and his narration is oblique—full of hypothetical constructions, opaque ironies, and peculiar self-refutations.

If the psychological interest of *Lovel* anticipates the modern novel, *Denis Duval* hearkens back to the older mode of romance. As if inspired by his Roundabout recollections of the swashbuckling novels he loved in his youth, Thackeray created in his last novel an exciting world of mystery and action. *Denis Duval* returns to the eighteenth century of *The Virginians,* but its pace is brisk, its characters fresh, and its narrator keeps his eye firmly on the story at hand. The absence of reflection and digression represents a conscious effort on Thackeray's part, as J. A. Sutherland has shown,[21] and it is all the more unusual given the autobiographical mode of the novel. Like Henry Esmond, Denis Duval tells his own story in old age, but his is a more straightforward psyche than that of Esmond. An unselfconscious man of action, Duval is distinguished by an early and firm sense of himself and his values. Characteristically, he loves only one woman and loves her—literally—from her infancy. Agnes de Saverne (later Duval) appears in Duval's life shortly after her birth when he is about six years old. The infant is brought from France to England by her deranged mother and the mother's reputed lover, later to be pursued by the Count, her father, in a chase that ends with his death in a duel. Duval's mother (a delightfully earthy woman) nurses the disturbed Countess, but the infant Agnes falls to the charge of Denis almost from the first and remains his love for life. Denis Duval, brought up among smugglers in an *emigré* French community in Winchelsea and exposed early to religious bigotry, deceit, highwaymen, and insanity, develops an independent spirit, joining the Navy at an early age, and he is about to engage in his first naval battle when the novel breaks off.

Thackeray completed about half of *Denis Duval* before his death, packing into its eight chapters more action than contained in the entire ninety-two chapters of *The Virginians*. Acutely aware of the dead ends and involutions to which his skeptical search for realism had brought him in works like *Lovel* and *Philip*, Thackeray altered his mode, accepting the "sweets" of romance and in so doing liberated the narrative energy blocked by his realist efforts. "How do you like your novels?" he asks in "De Finibus." "I like mine strong, 'hot with,' and no mistake; no love-making: no observations about society: little dialogue, except where the characters are bullying each other: plenty of fighting: and a villain in the cupboard, who is to suffer tortures just before Finis." As his own Finis, *Denis Duval* is an invigorated conclusion.

Chapter Eight
Conclusion

To read Thackeray is to encounter a slippery, skeptical intelligence whose fiction denies the pleasures of surrender to another world and refuses the consolations inherent in the pattern-making power of the imagination. Insisting on the responsibility of fiction to life but finally unsure whether this commitment is not itself a delusion, Thackeray's novels are disquieting, often exasperating, and always provocative. His devious texts compel the reader's engagement, raising important questions about the assumptions that inform our interpretation of life as well as of narratives. In this ability to provoke thought lies Thackeray's enduring achievement, an achievement linked directly (if sometimes paradoxically) to his allegiance to the powerful realist model of the novel that dominated the nineteenth century.[1]

Realism itself is something of a paradox: a literary mode that attempts to deny its own status as literature. Seeking to erase the distinction between life and art, realism assumes that literature can be a mirror on empirical reality, but this confidence is threatened by its simultaneous awareness that there is always a gap between literature and the world it imitates. On the surface, realism exploits that gap to authenticate its own texts. From Cervantes on, realist writers have traditionally bolstered the truthfulness of their own narratives by discrediting other narratives as foolish romances or mere conventional structures.[2] So to establish the realism of his first novel, Thackeray in *Catherine* attacks other novels, his exposure of the sentimental artifices of Newgate fiction heightening the authority of the brutal counterworld he has created in his own fiction. But such a strategy makes all novels vulnerable, as Thackeray well knew. Even in his own career *Henry Esmond* came to seem an impossible dream by the time of *The Virginians,* and Thackeray would be the first to appreciate the irony that where Victorian readers saw realism, later generations would find sentimentality.

Thackeray never abandoned the realist desire to make art correspond to life, but he was more acutely aware than most of his contemporaries of the precariousness of the enterprise, alert to the inherent strains and contradictions in realism, playing with its assumptions and probing its limits. Even as Thackeray's narrators pretend (again following the example of Cervantes) that they are not writing novels at all but actual biographies and histories, they expose their own pretense. The obviously fallible Pen of *Philip* ironically assumes the character of "infallible historian," and the narrator of *Vanity Fair* explains scrupulously his reliance on gossip for information only to explode the whole pose by then revealing himself as the puppet-master controlling the entire fiction. Such moments typify the way that Thackeray's narrative draws attention to the conventions that make possible our serious reading of fiction and calls into question the authority of narrators, historians—even of puppet-masters. As evasive and purposeless as such moments may sometimes become in their particular context, they grow out of Thackeray's general commitment to truth and his conviction that truth is always difficult and always partial. "No human brain is big enough to grasp the whole truth," he wrote in 1857, "—and mine can take in no doubt but a very infinitesimal portion of it but such truth as I know that I must tell" (*Letters,* 4:14).[3]

Such truth as Thackeray knew was truth of experience, not of essence: historical rather than philosophical, empirical rather than transcendental. And it was his fidelity to the truths of experience that earned him his reputation among his contemporaries. His willingness to include "disagreeable truths," for example, led George Eliot to comment at the outset of her own novelistic career that she considered Thackeray "as I suppose the majority of people with any intellect do, on the whole the most powerful of living novelists."[4] Writing to his sister just a few days before Thackeray died, the young Thomas Hardy defined both Thackeray's status and its source: "He is considered to be the greatest novelist of the day—looking at novel writing of the highest kind as a perfect and truthful representation of actual life."[5] Not all agreed that such writing was indeed "of the highest kind," seeing in realism a tendency to cynicism or to moral ambiguity incompatible with their sense of high art. "We cannot see our way clearly," a Victorian reviewer said of *Vanity Fair,* because its characters "are too like our every-day selves to draw any distinct moral from."[6] Other readers objected to the social focus of realism itself as offering a narrow and superficial interpretation of human life but testified to the power of Thackeray's realist illusion. "Many novelists have a world of their own which they inhabit," W. C. Roscoe wrote. "Thackeray thrusts his characters in among the moving every-day world in which we live."[7]

The world in which Thackeray's characters live is predominantly middle-class. Although he ranges over the social scale to include laundresses and lords, his focus is on the urban, mercantile class rapidly gaining ascendance in Victorian society. Its displacement of the aristocracy meant an important shift in the social power base from land to money, a liquid asset that is anonymous, easily transferable, and unstable. Breaking up the old hierarchies, money creates a more mobile society marked by rapid, often unpredictable movements up and down the social scale. In the mobile Becky Sharp—clawing her way up, tumbling down, and regrouping to try again—Thackeray created a superb emblem for the new, fluid world emerging in his time. He is the great English novelist of money, choosing as his controlling metaphor for society the image of a market, Vanity Fair, where everything is for sale, where traditional categories of value have dissolved, where all is in motion. Markets contain energy and excitement as well as deceit and emptiness, and Thackeray's power as an analyst of a money society owes as much to his knowledge of its attractions as to his awareness of its confusions and hollowness.

As John Carey has demonstrated, Thackeray's concrete imagination has a strong hedonistic strain, expressing a sensuous delight in food and drink, in shiny surfaces and beautiful textures.[8] Particularly in his early work, his "fluent, darting genius" (the phrase is Carey's) works in a rapid, impressionistic manner to capture the evanescent pleasures of the world. "It is all vanity to be sure," comments the narrator of *Vanity Fair,* "but who will not own to liking a little of it? I should like to know what well-constituted mind, merely because it is transitory, dislikes roast beef?" (ch. 51). In *Vanity Fair,* and to a lesser extent in *Pendennis,* Thackeray conveys the vitality and glitter of a society on the move, recording with humor and insight the dependence of civilized society on its material context. Thackeray's world is physically dense, full of chairs, clocks, pianos, pictures, mirrors, shawls, boots, and buttons.[9] Recognizing the power of objects, their emotional resonance as well as physical presence, Thackeray penetrated their significance in human life more acutely than any other Victorian writer. The Sedleys of *Vanity Fair* witness the way in which things define people and people define themselves through things, as the once genial parents, deprived of the things that supported their status, degenerate into meanness and self-deception, as Amelia turns George's picture into an icon supporting her fantasy of herself, and Jos labors vainly to believe in himself by stuffing his bulky body into elaborate waistcoats and polished boots.

Thackeray's mastery of the small, signifying gesture—Becky choking on chili peppers, Dobbin carrying Amelia's shawl, George buying a diamond shirt-pin—points to the subtle intelligence informing his diagnosis of the culture in which he participated. Where his great rival, Charles Dickens, working in a different mode, created large, dramatic effects to indict the injustices of Victorian society, Thackeray chose to focus on its hypocrisies and relied typically on indirection, irony, and the accumulation of suggestive details. His analysis of snobbery, the form of hypocrisy characteristic of an insecure middle class recently emancipated from aristocratic rule, made him famous.

But Thackeray saw hypocrisy as more insidious and pervasive than in its manifestation of snobbery. His novels, most notably *The Newcomes,* imply that the entire social structure is not only permeated with but built on shams and pretensions (conscious and unconscious) that infect both private and public life. The marriage market (even marriage itself) trains women to hypocrisy from birth, while the powerful code of respectability, as exemplified by Barnes Newcome, is founded on maintaining the appearance of moral values contradicted by actual actions and motives. Expanding the insight of *Vanity Fair,* where not being found out was more important than being innocent, *The Newcomes* exposes a society based on a divergence between word and act, reputation and truth, where individuals absorb contradictory codes of conduct that operate simultaneously. But Thackeray pushes further, beyond social analysis, to question whether hypocrisy may not be endemic to the human condition: "With the very first page of the human story do not love, and lies too, begin?" (*Newcomes,* ch. 1). Entangled in deceptions and self-deceptions from the time of Eden, he suggests, humanity inherits a contradictory nature that makes hypocrisy inevitable.

The expanding focus of the theme of hypocrisy from the specific phenomenon of snobbery to the general structure of society to perennial existential conditions illustrates how Thackeray's mind probed questions, his realist desire to understand the life of his time leading him beyond the conventional limits of social realism. Impelled by the restless mind and the brooding sensibility underlying his gregarious, hedonistic impulses, Thackeray moved behind surfaces, beneath the "subsoil of life" which Walter Bagehot declared to be his territory, to the deeper layers of human reality.[10] In *The Newcomes* Thackeray presents the novelist as excavator, an archeologist or paleontologist digging among ruins, uncovering remnants. But the novelist excavates contemporary life, and in his own uncovering Thackeray discovered the dark, predatory forces feeding civilized existence. Exchanging the referential language of realism for the opacity of metaphor and allusion, his novels weave in images of cannibalism, violence, and murder to hint at the disturbing underside of the Victorian world, an underside that threatens in *Philip* to explode the social surfaces of the fiction. *Henry Esmond* works with the complex tensions of personal relationships controlled by irrational forces that are dimly recognized, deeply resented, and culturally forbidden. Thackeray's novels are always alert to the psychological and emotional consequences of powerful cultural myths, as in his continuing scrutiny of woman as angel, from the fixated Amelia to the smothering Helen Pendennis to the tormented and jealous Rachel Esmond. In the oppressive mothers, oedipal sons, foolish wives, bored husbands, and impotent fathers of his fiction Thackeray suggests the debilitating effects of the Victorian worship of domesticity even as he yearns for its comforts.

The domestic dream was all the more appealing, for Thackeray's skeptical exploration of Victorian reality revealed to him a contingent universe, a world without a center of meaning, governed by the relentless passage of time which brings with it only decay and death. It is a modern sense of reality, and Thackeray's novels are haunted by a modern cluster of themes: the subjectivity of reality, the isolation of the individual, the problem of time, the centrality of memory. "You and I are but a pair of infinite isolations," notes the narrator of *Pendennis* (ch. 16), and *The Newcomes* elaborates the perception in its extended metaphor of life as a voyage in which ships cross without necessarily connecting (ch. 24). Life is contingency, ruled by the chances and changes of time which threaten to erode even the belief in the continuity of the self. Remembering his college days, the narrator of *Pendennis* asks: "are we the same men now that wrote those inscriptions?" (ch. 18). The question motivates Henry Esmond's entire narrative, and he returns a positive answer, insisting that memory does in fact affirm the identity of his being. *The Virginians* suggests that Esmond's memory may be as much refuge as recovery, as much illusion as discovery. But memory is all that an individual has in the disenchanted Thackerayan world, and Thackeray explores its workings from the outset of his career, anticipating as early as *Barry Lyndon* Proust's famous involuntary memory and subjecting to a continuing rich musing the truths and deceptions of our remembering.[11]

Increasingly in Thackeray's fiction the subjective conditions of experience become the locus of interest, bringing him, as John Loofbourow has shown, closer to the early modernists than to contemporaries like Dickens.[12] Although Thackeray never denied the significance of social forms or rejected the external world, his exploratory realism brought him toward a relativistic, psychological definition of reality that was contained uneasily within traditional forms of narrative. He virtually abandoned plot after *The Newcomes* as inescapably fictitious, throwing up his hands at the end of that novel and allowing the reader to complete the story as he or she desired. As *Philip* makes clear, the reliance of plot on external event obscures the motives that matter, and its linearity fails to take into account the important nonlinearities of life. Faithful to realism's suspicion of literature, Thackeray was a highly self-conscious artist, applying to the forms of fiction (including his own) the same scrutiny as to the forms of life.

His concern remained always the realist concern with the adequacy and truthfulness of his own telling. His narrators question themselves, rejecting Victorian omniscience whose assumptions about direct, objective knowledge Thackeray could not accept. More thoroughly than any of his contemporaries, he made his readers aware that literature is a mediation, its processes depending upon convention. Realism as language transparent on and coextensive with the world he came to recognize as impossible. But by admitting its impossibility, perhaps a truth could be salvaged, a hypocrisy—in his own sense of the term—avoided. Thackeray's special integrity led him finally to undermine the strategies of his own fiction in the disturbing, self-reflexive novels of his late period. But in his continuing struggle to make the novel responsible to existential reality, he opened up Victorian fiction, established both its realism and the limits of that realism, and raised important questions about the nature of narrative which continue to compel attention and to elude definition.

Notes and References

Chapter One

1. "De Finibus," *Roundabout Papers.* Since there is no standard edition of Thackeray's works, quotations from the novels will be identified by chapter in the text; in shorter works where there are no chapters, the title of the piece will be cited. The edition I quote throughout (except where specified) is the Library Edition, *The Works of William Makepeace Thackeray,* 24 vols. (London, 1867–69, 1886).

2. *Letters and Private Papers of William Makepeace Thackeray,* ed. Gordon N. Ray, 4 vols. (Cambridge, Mass., 1945–46), 2:815; hereafter cited as *Letters* in the text.

3. My discussion is based on the definitive two-volume biography of Thackeray by Gordon N. Ray, *Thackeray: The Uses of Adversity, 1811–1846* and *Thackeray: The Age of Wisdom, 1847–1863* (New York, 1955, 1958); hereafter cited as *Uses of Adversity* and *Age of Wisdom.*

4. MS. letter, July 1820, quoted in Ray, *Uses of Adversity,* p. 75.

5. Gordon N. Ray, *The Buried Life: A Study of the Relation Between Thackeray's Fiction and His Personal History* (Cambridge, Mass.: Harvard University Press, 1952), p. 14.

6. For a discussion of Thackeray's tendency to create "masks" for self-protection see Lambert Ennis, *Thackeray: The Sentimental Cynic* (Evanston, 1950), pp. 2–4.

7. *Letters of Thomas Carlyle, 1826–1836,* ed. Charles Eliot Norton, 2 vols. (London: Macmillan, 1887), 1:283.

8. Ennis, *Sentimental Cynic,* p. 73.

9. For an influential interpretation of the positive significance of the family reunion see Gordon N. Ray, "*Vanity Fair*: One Version of the Novelist's Responsibility," *Essays by Divers Hands: Being the Transactions of the Royal Society of Literature In the United Kingdom,* n.s. 25 (1950): 87–101. The essay is reprinted in *The Victorian Novel: Modern Essays in Criticism,* ed. Ian Watt (London: Oxford University Press, 1971), pp. 248–65. More recently, John Carey has offered an opposing view of Thackeray's life and work in *Thackeray: Prodigal Genius* (London, 1977).

Chapter Two

1. *Spectator,* July 18, 1840, and [G. H. Lewes], *Morning Chronicle,* March 6, 1848, reprinted in *Thackeray: The Critical Heritage,* ed. Geoffrey Tillotson and Donald Hawes (London, 1968), pp. 25, 44–49; hereafter cited as *Critical Heritage.*

2. James H. Wheatley, *Patterns in Thackeray's Fiction* (Cambridge, Mass., 1969), p. 6.

3. For a discusion of the Newgate novel and Thackeray's part in the controversy see Keith Hollingsworth, *The Newgate Novel 1830–1847* (Detroit: Wayne State University Press, 1963).

4. Thackeray, "Horae Catnachianae," *Fraser's Magazine* 19 (April 1839): 407–24.

5. Edward Lytton Bulwer, *Eugene Aram* (New York: Harper, 1836), bk. 5, ch. 7, pp. 179, 185. The novel went through various revisions and this edition contains the original text.

6. Dedication to 1845 ed. of *Zanoni* (1842), [*Lytton's Novels*], 25 vols. (London: Routledge, 1877–78), 25:vi.

7. For a discussion of the relationship between Thackeray's theories of painting and literature, see Robert A. Colby, *Thackeray's Canvass of Humanity* (Columbus, 1979), pp. 57–86.

8. *Zanoni,* bk. 2, ch. 9, pp. 116–17.

9. The account of Catherine Hayes is found in Andrew Knapp and William Baldwin, *The New Newgate Calendar,* 5. vols (London: J & J. Cundee, [1824–26]), 1:347–64.

10. This is especially true of the original version of the novel serialized in *Fraser's.* Later editions omit details of the murder, the death of Catherine, and some specific hits at the fashion for Newgate stories. The original version may be found in *The Oxford Thackeray,* ed. George Saintsbury, 17 vols (London, 1908), vol. 3. Jack Sheppard was the hero of the most popular Newgate novel, William Harrison Ainsworth's *Jack Sheppard* (1839), to which Thackeray refers in *Catherine.*

11. See "The Case of Peytel" (1839) in *Paris Sketch Book* and "Going to See a Man Hanged," *Fraser's* 22 (Aug. 1840): 150–58.

12. *Fors Clavigera,* Letter 31 in *The Works of John Ruskin,* ed. E. T. Cook and Alexander Wedderburn, 39 vols (London: George Allen, 1903–1912), 27: 562.

13. The most useful edition of the novel is the critical edition edited by Martin J. Anisman, *The Luck of Barry Lyndon* (New York: New York University Press, 1970). Anisman restores the original text and chapter numbers, making clear which passages were omitted in later editions. He also includes a helpful discussion of historical sources for the figure of the hero. My chapter references are based on this edition.

14. See Colby, *Canvass of Humanity,* pp. 209–15.

15. Complaints about writing *Barry Lyndon* are scattered throughout the 1844 diary, *Letters,* 1:139–57.

16. Anthony Trollope, *Thackeray* (1879; reprinted, London: Macmillan, 1906), p. 70.

17. My citations are to this later, shorter version found in most collected editions of Thackeray. The original *Punch* text may be found in *The Book of Snobs,* ed. John Sutherland (New York: St. Martin's Press, 1978). This edition contains a valuable introduction and notes.

18. *Morning Chronicle,* March 6, 1848, in *Critical Heritage,* p. 49.

19. Introduction to *The Book of Snobs* (London, 1911) quoted in Ray, *Uses of Adversity,* p. 377.

20. Ray, *Uses of Adversity,* pp. 13–14.

Chapter Three

1. See Kathleen Tillotson, *Novels of the Eighteen-Forties* (London: Oxford University Press, 1956), pp. 25–53, for a general analysis of the importance of part publication for the Victorian novel. References in this chapter are to the standard modern edition of *Vanity Fair,* ed. Geoffrey and Kathleen Tillotson (Boston: Houghton Mifflin, 1963).

2. John Harvey discusses Thackeray as illustrator in *Victorian Novelists and Their Illustrators* (New York: New York University Press; London: Sidgwick & Jackson, 1970), pp. 76–102.

3. See Joan Stevens, "Thackeray's *Vanity Fair,*" *Review of English Literature* 6 (1965): 19–38, and Teona Tone Gneiting, "The Pencil's Role in *Vanity Fair,*" *Huntington Library Quarterly* 39 (1976): 171–202.

4. For an analysis of Thackeray's skill as a serial novelist see Edgar F. Harden, "The Discipline and Significance of Form in *Vanity Fair,*" *PMLA* 82 (1967): 530–41.

5. [R.S. Rintoul], *Spectator,* July 22, 1848, in *Critical Heritage,* p. 59.

6. Elizabeth Rigby, *"Vanity Fair—and Jane Eyre,"* *Quarterly Review* (Dec. 1848), in *Critical Heritage,* p. 79,

7. Robert Bell, *Fraser's Magazine* (Sep. 1848), in *Critical Heritage,* pp. 64–65.

8. G. K. Chesterton, *A Handful of Authors* (London: Sheed & Ward, 1953), p. 61.

9. I quote the Signet edition of *The Pilgrim's Progress* (New York: New American Library, 1964), p. 84.

10. The darker strains of *Vanity Fair*—its sense of the irrational and violent forces underlying civilization—have recently received some perceptive critical attention. See in particular Robert E. Lougy, "Vision and Satire: The Warped Looking Glass in *Vanity Fair,*" *PMLA* 90 (1975): 256–69, and Maria Di-Battista, "The Triumph of Clytemnestra: The Charades in *Vanity Fair,*" *PMLA* 95 (1980): 827–37.

11. See, for example, the important essay by G. Armour Craig, "On the Style of *Vanity Fair*," in *Style in Prose Fiction,* ed. Harold C. Martin. English Institute Essays (New York, 1959), pp. 87–113. The essay is widely reprinted in collections on the Victorian novel and on Thackeray, including *Thackeray: A Collection of Critical Essays,* ed. Alexander Welsh (Englewood Cliffs, N.J., 1968).

12. Ann Y. Wilkinson, "The Tomeavsian Way of Knowing the World: Technique and Meaning in *Vanity Fair,* " *ELH* 32 (1965): 377.

13. Wolfgang Iser analyzes the active role of the reader in *Vanity Fair* in *The Implied Reader* (Baltimore, 1974), pp. 101–20.

14. Juliet M. McMaster, *Thackeray: The Major Novels* (Toronto, 1971), p. 1. See Chapter 1 for an extended analysis of the function of the narrator.

15. A. E. Dyson, "Thackeray: An Irony Against Heroes," in his *The Crazy Fabric* (London: Macmillan, 1965), p. 76.

16. Jack P. Rawlins, *Thackeray's Novels: A Fiction That Is True* (Berkeley, 1974), p. 10.

17. My analysis of the episode draws on U.C. Knoepflmacher, *Laughter and Despair* (Berkeley, 1971), pp. 66–71, and Rawlins, *Thackeray's Novels,* pp. 4–12.

18. Letter to W. S. Williams, Aug. 14, 1848, in *Critical Heritage,* p. 52.

19. For a summary of critical response to Becky see John Hagan, "*Vanity Fair*: Becky Brought to Book Again," *Studies in the Novel* 7 (1975): 479–505.

20. See Rawlins, *Thackeray's Novels,* pp. 30–35.

21. Dyson, *The Crazy Fabric,* p. 94.

22. For a perceptive psychological analysis of the relationship between Dobbin and Amelia see Bernard J. Paris, "The Psychic Structure of *Vanity Fair*" in his *A Psychological Approach to Fiction* (Bloomington, Ind., 1974), pp. 106–14.

23. See Alexander Welsh, "The Allegory of Truth in English Fiction," *Victorian Studies* 9 (1965): 1–27.

Chapter Four

1. Ray's *The Buried Life* is devoted to an analysis of the relations between Thackeray's life and his fiction; *Pendennis* is discussed on pp. 48–77. The Penguin English Library edition of *The History of Pendennis,* ed. Donald Hawes (Harmondsworth, Middlesex: Penguin, 1972) provides a list identifying the sources of people and places in the novel. All my chapter references are to this edition which incorporates the 1856 revisions of *Pendennis.*

2. See Ennis, *Sentimental Cynic,* pp. 156–57, for an analysis of how Thackeray's ambivalent response to his mother influences the characterization of Helen Pendennis.

3. For an introduction to the *Bildungsroman* see Jerome Hamilton Buckley, *Season of Youth: The Bildungsroman from Dickens to Golding* (Cambridge, Mass.:

Harvard University Press, 1974), ch. 1. Buckley admits that *Pendennis* has many elements of the *Bildungsroman* but dismisses it from his discussion for reasons that are not entirely clear (pp. 28–30). See also Winslow Rogers, "Thackeray's Self-Consciousness" in *The Worlds of Victorian Fiction,* ed. Jerome H. Buckley (Cambridge, Mass.: Harvard University Press, 1975), pp. 154–55. Rogers finds that Thackeray has a static concept of character that precludes him from creating the sense of development essential to the *Bildungsroman.*

4. Wheatley, *Patterns in Thackeray's Fiction,* pp. 96–103, considers some of the general thematic implications of Thackeray's use of "the young tyro" as the structural center of his novels.

5. J.A. Sutherland, *Thackeray at Work* (London, 1974), ch. 2, shows how Thackeray uses Pen's novel to raise questions about the relationship between autobiography and fiction.

6. W.C. Roscoe, "W.M. Thackeray, Artist and Moralist," *National Review* (Jan. 1856), in *Critical Heritage,* p. 272.

7. Ibid., p. 278.

8. Bulwer-Lytton, *England and the English,* ed. Standish Meacham (Chicago: University of Chicago Press, 1970), p. 318. Bulwer first published this work in 1833; my quotation is from Book 4, ch. 6.

9. *The Life of John Sterling* in *The Works of Thomas Carlyle,* ed. H. D. Traill, 30 vols (London: Chapman & Hall, 1897–99), 11:96.

10. *Arnold: Poetical Works,* ed. C.B. Tinker and H.F. Lowry (London: Oxford University Press, 1950), p. 302.

11. A useful introduction to the politics, religion, and social order of Victorian England is J. B. Schneewind, *Backgrounds of English Victorian Literature* (New York: Random House, 1970).

12. Fitzjames Stephen, "The Relation of Novels to Life" in *Cambridge Essays, Contributed by Members of the University, 1855–1857* (London: J. W. Parker, 1855), 1:184.

13. *An Essay on Criticism* (1711), ll. 70–71, *The Poems of Alexander Pope,* ed. John Butt (London: Methuen, 1965), p. 146.

14. I refer to the title page of the first volume of the first bound edition. In the drawing for the serial version the choice represented by the female figure is even more apparent, though Pen's decision is less clear. For a discussion of the differences between the two illustrations see Jean Sudrann, " 'The Philosopher's Property': Thackeray and the Use of Time," *Victorian Studies* 10 (1967): 365–68.

15. See Edgar F. Harden, "Theatricality in *Pendennis,*" *Ariel* 4 (1973): 74–94.

16. John Loofbourow, *Thackeray and the Form of Fiction* (Princeton, 1964), p. 53. See also pp. 57–60.

17. Barbara Hardy, *The Exposure of Luxury: Radical Themes in Thackeray* (Pittsburgh, 1972), p. 86.

18. For an excellent discussion of Thackeray's attitude to time, including a

discussion of *Pendennis,* see Jean Sudrann, " 'The Philosopher's Property': Thackeray and the Use of Time."

19. Alexander Welsh, *The City of Dickens* (Oxford: Clarendon Press, 1971), Part 3, analyzes the nature and function of the Victorian heroine. See also Walter E. Houghton's chapter on love in his *The Victorian Frame of Mind, 1830–70* (New Haven: Yale University Press, 1957), pp. 341–83.

20. J. Hillis Miller, *The Form of Victorian Fiction* (Notre Dame, Ind., 1968), p. 96.

21. Houghton, *Victorian Frame of Mind,* p. 344.

22. Robert Bledsoe, *"Pendennis* and the Power of Sentimentality: A Study of Motherly Love," *PMLA* 91 (1976): 881. Bledsoe provides a penetrating analysis of the implications of Thackeray's handling of Helen Pendennis. See also Thomas L. Jeffers, "Thackeray's Pendennis: Son and Gentleman," *Nineteenth-Century Fiction* 33 (1978): 175–93.

Chapter Five

1. The novel's full title appears on the original title page which is reproduced in the Penguin English Library edition of *The History of Henry Esmond,* ed. John Sutherland and Michael Greenfield (Harmondsworth, Middlesex: Penguin, 1970). This edition, including a useful introduction by Sutherland and notes, is the basis of all my references.

2. "Thackeray's New Novel," *Leader,* Nov. 6, 1852, in *Critical Heritage,* p. 136.

3. Review in *Examiner,* Nov. 13, 1852, in *Critical Heritage,* p. 145.

4. [Samuel Phillips], "Mr. Thackeray's New Novel," *Times,* Dec. 22, 1852, in *Critical Heritage,* p. 155. Thackeray later claimed that this review "absolutely stopped" sales of *Henry Esmond, Letters,* 4:125.

5. Ray provides an authoritative account of the Brookfield affair and shows its impact on *Henry Esmond* in *Age of Wisdom,* pp. 58–91; 157–67; 180–89.

6. *Critical Heritage,* p. 137.

7. *The George Eliot Letters,* ed. Gordon S. Haight, 7 vols (New Haven: Yale University Press, 1954–55), 2:67.

8. *Athenaeum,* November 6, 1852, p. 1199; [Margaret Oliphant], "Mr. Thackeray and his Novels," *Blackwood's Magazine* (Jan. 1855), in *Critical Heritage,* p. 209.

9. James Thomas Fields, *Yesterdays With Authors* (Boston: Houghton Mifflin, 1900), p. 17.

10. Trollope, *Thackeray,* p. 124.

11. For the importance of retrospection in creating Esmond's sense of self see Henri-A. Talon, "Time and Memory in Thackeray's *Henry Esmond,*" *Review of English Studies* 13 (1962): 147–56. See also Edgar F. Harden, "Esmond and the Search for Self," *Yearbook of English Studies* 3 (1973): 181–95.

12. Miller, *Form of Victorian Fiction*, p. 97. See pp. 97–104 for an analysis of the novel's oedipal patterns.

13. For a psychological reading of the novel stressing the theme of fathers and sons see Sylvia Manning, "Incest and the Structure of *Henry Esmond*," *Nineteenth-Century Fiction* 34 (1979):194–213.

14. Loofbourow, *Thackeray and the Form of Fiction*, p. 133. Loofbourow provides an excellent discussion of the epic significance of *Henry Esmond*, pp. 118–61.

15. See *Letters*, 4:209, 236. Thackeray paid tribute to Macaulay in the Roundabout Paper, "Nil Nisi Bonum."

16. Macaulay, *History of England From the Accession of James II*, 9th ed., 5 vols (London: Longman, Brown, 1853), 1:1, 3.

17. Avrom Fleishman argues that Esmond moves finally beyond history itself toward an ideal of life outside history in *The English Historical Novel: Walter Scott to Virginia Woolf* (Baltimore: Johns Hopkins University Press, 1971), pp. 142–46.

18. Thomas Carlyle, "On History," *Critical and Miscellaneous Essays*, 3d ed., 4 vols (London: Chapman & Hall, 1847), 1:152.

19. José Ortega y Gasset, *History as a System*, trans. Helene Weyl (1941; reprint ed., New York: Norton, 1961), p. 214.

20. Georg Lukacs, *The Historical Novel*, trans. Hannah and Stanley Mitchell (Harmondsworth, Middlesex: Penguin, 1962), p. 15.

21. Thomas Carlyle, "On History Again," *Critical and Miscellaneous Essays*, 3:191.

22. Jane Millgate, "History *versus* Fiction: Thackeray's Response to Macaulay," *Costerus*, n.s. 2 (1974): 43–58, discusses Thackeray's ideas on the relationship between history and fiction.

23. McMaster, *Thackeray: The Major Novels*, p. 122. See also Miller, *Form of Victorian Fiction*, pp. 23–34, 101–104, for an account of how Esmond sets himself up as a god.

24. John Sutherland regards this editorial apparatus as a late, brilliant improvisation arising from Thackeray's growing scruples as a historian over his portrait of Marlborough, *Thackeray at Work*, pp. 66–73. The more traditional view of the novel as carefully planned and revised is to be found in Ray, *Age of Wisdom*, p. 176.

Chapter Six

1. *Times*, Aug. 29, 1855, in *Critical Heritage*, p. 223. The most accessible edition of *The Newcomes* is the Everyman Library edition (London: Dent, 1910), 2 vols. All references are to this edition which, unfortunately, does not include the illustrations.

2. Ray, *Age of Wisdom*, p. 247.

3. *Critical Heritage*, p. 227, 211.

4. Despite modern dislike of the Victorian death scene, the death of Colonel Newcome continues to be much admired. See, for example, Sutherland, *Thackeray at Work*, pp. 80–85.

5. James Wheatley is skeptical about the quixotic allusions in *The Newcomes* because "the subject and resulting book are so unlike that of Cervantes," *Patterns in Thackeray's Fiction*, p. 115.

6. José Ortega y Gasset, *Meditations on Quixote*, trans. Evelyn Rugg and Diego Marin (New York: Norton, 1961), p. 162.

7. R. D. McMaster, "The Pygmalion Motif in *The Newcomes*," *Nineteenth-Century Fiction* 29 (1974):22.

8. Robert Colby discusses the military conduct book by J. H. Stocqueler, *The British Officer: His Positions, Duties, Emoluments and Privileges* (1851) in the context of *The Newcomes*, in *Thackeray's Canvass of Humanity*, pp. 365–67.

9. Thackeray himself reread *Don Quixote* while he was writing *The Newcomes* and commented: "What a vitality in those two characters [Don Quixote and Sancho Panza]! What gentlemen they both are!" *Letters*, 3:304.

10. The narrator of *The Newcomes* is actually Thackeray's old hero, Arthur Pendennis, whom Thackeray regarded as a "mask" allowing him "to say and think many things that I couldn't venture on in my own person, now that it is a person, and I know the public are staring at it" (*Letters*, 4:436). Because Pendennis (in this novel at least) is clearly an alter ego and functions pretty much like the third-person narrators of previous novels, I present him throughout the chapter as simply "the narrator."

11. McMaster, *Thackeray: The Major Novels*, p. 155.

12. Juliet McMaster distinguishes between two kinds of animal imagery: one type evokes a moral universe, the other an amoral world, *Thackeray: The Major Novels*, pp. 173–74.

13. *Quarterly Review* (Sept. 1855), in *Critical Heritage*, p. 247. See also Jenni Calder who finds that Thackeray categorizes women in terms of submission or rebellion and judges both types to be destructive, *Women and Marriage in Victorian Fiction* (London: Thames & Hudson, 1976), pp. 27–55.

14. Katharine M. Rogers is not persuaded by Ethel's unconventionality, arguing that Thackeray's women become more conventional after *Vanity Fair*, "The Pressure of Convention on Thackeray's Women," *Modern Language Review* 67 (1972):257–63.

15. This paragraph draws on a more extended discussion of Thackeray's modification of the convention of the heroine in my "The Demystification of Laura Pendennis," *Studies in the Novel* 13 (1981): 122–32.

16. For the role of fictions in the novel, see R.D. McMaster, "The Pygmalion Motif in *The Newcomes*."

17. McMaster, *Thackeray: The Major Novels*, p. 165.

18. Sudrann, "'The Philosopher's Property': Thackeray and the Use of Time," p. 379.

19. Roscoe, "W.M. Thackeray, Artist and Moralist," in *Critical Heritage*, p. 280.

20. Joan Garret-Goodyear demonstrates how Thackeray's characterization in *The Newcomes* and *Henry Esmond* conveys the sense of frustrated passionate impulse, citing Rosey Mackenzie as one of her examples, "Stylized Emotions, Unrealized Selves: Expressive Characterization in Thackeray," *Victorian Studies* 22 (1979): 173–92.

21. Preface to *The Tragic Muse*, reprinted in Henry James, *The Art of the Novel* (New York: Scribner's, 1934), p. 84. R. D. McMaster traces the influence of *The Newcomes* on the early James in "'An Honorable Emulation of the Author of *The Newcomes*': James and Thackeray," *Nineteenth-Century Fiction* 32 (1978): 399–419.

Chapter Seven

1. All references to Thackeray's work in this chapter are to the Library Edition of the *Works* (cited in the Notes to Chapter 1) since there are no readily available separate editions of his later writings. I have, however, numbered the chapters sequentially.

2. Goldwin Smith, *Edinburgh Review* (Oct. 1859), in *Critical Heritage*, p. 292.

3. Walter Bagehot, *Spectator,* Aug. 9, 1862, in *Critical Heritage*, p. 306.

4. *Saturday Review,* Aug. 23, 1862, in *Critical Heritage*, p. 310.

5. For some of the complexities of Thackeray's handling of the old versus new theme, see Gerald C. Sorensen, "Beginning and Ending: *The Virginians* as a Sequel," *Studies in the Novel* 13 (1981): 109–21.

6. Juliet McMaster points out that the history of the Esmond family in *Henry Esmond* and *The Virginians* is "a prolonged account of the mating of different generations" in her discussion of "ambivalent relationships" in Thackeray's novels, *Thackeray: The Major Novels,* p. 215.

7. Rawlins, *Thackeray's Novels,* p. 190. I am indebted to Rawlins's stimulating approach to *The Virginians.*

8. Ibid., p. 201.

9. Robert L. Caserio, *Plot, Story and the Novel* (Princeton: Princeton University Press, 1979), p. xiii.

10. Gordon Ray discusses the identification between Thackeray and his late narrators in *Age of Wisdom*, pp. 373–75. For a consideration of Thackeray's complicated self-scrutiny in *Philip*, see Juliet McMaster, "Funeral Baked Meats: Thackeray's Last Novel," *Studies in the Novel* 13 (1981): 133–55.

11. See Joseph P. Baker, "*The Adventures of Philip*" reprinted in Alexander

Welsh, ed., *Thackeray: A Collection of Critical Essays,* pp. 161–77. The essay appeared originally as "Thackeray's Recantation," *PMLA* 77 (1962): 586–94. See also Rawlins, *Thackeray's Novels,* pp. 219–24.

12. For a more psychological interpretation of Philip's career, see my "Narrative Strategy in Thackeray's *The Adventures of Philip,*" *English Studies in Canada* 5 (1979): 448–56.

13. Colby, *Thackeray's Canvass of Humanity,* p. 438.

14. Rawlins makes the same point but concentrates on the moral implications of the devaluation of plot, stressing that when meaning no longer lies in action, the moral link between action and consequence is broken. Philip, for example, is continually freed from the consequences of his actions, *Thackeray's Novels,* pp. 215–20.

15. Baker, *"The Adventures of Philip,"* in Welsh, *Collection of Critical Essays,* p. 163.

16. Juliet McMaster, "Funeral Baked Meats: Thackeray's Last Novel," p. 138.

17. See Miller, *Form of Victorian Fiction,* p. 67.

18. For a discussion of the problem of mediation see the chapter on Thackeray in Peter K. Garrett, *The Victorian Multiplot Novel: Studies in Dialogical Form* (New Haven, 1980). Garrett discusses Pen as narrator of *The Newcomes,* pp. 130–31. For a more extended analysis of Pen as the personalized narrator of *Philip,* see my "Narrative Strategy in Thackeray's *The Adventures of Philip.*"

19. For a fine discussion on memory in the Roundabouts to which I am indebted, see Richard W. Oram, "'Just a Little Turn of the Circle': Time, Memory, and Repetition in Thackeray's *Roundabout Papers,*" *Studies in the Novel* 13 (1981):156–67.

20. David L. James, "Story and Substance in *Lovel the Widower,*" *Journal of Narrative Technique* 7 (1977): 70–79. See also my "The Breakdown of Thackeray's Narrator: *Lovel the Widower,*" *Nineteenth-Century Fiction* 32 (1977): 36–53.

21. Sutherland, *Thackeray at Work,* pp. 120–24.

Chapter Eight

1. The current renewal of critical interest in realism has revived serious consideration of Thackeray, as demonstrated in George Levine's recent study, *The Realistic Imagination* (Chicago, 1981). In his three chapters on Thackeray, Levine offers a penetrating analysis of Thackeray's complex understanding of realism. Regrettably, this fine study appeared too late for me to draw on it as I would have wished.

2. Harry Levin defines this technique of realism in *The Gates of Horn* (New York: Oxford University Press, 1963), pp. 43–48.

3. See also Thackeray's Preface to *Pendennis* where he addresses the reader: "I ask you to believe that this person writing strives to tell the truth. If there is not that there is nothing."

4. *George Eliot Letters,* 2:349.

5. *The Collected Letters of Thomas Hardy,* ed. Richard Little Purdy and Michael Millgate (Oxford: Clarendon, 1978), 1:5.

6. Elizabeth Rigby, *"Vanity Fair—and Jane Eyre,"* in *Critical Heritage,* p. 80.

7. Roscoe, "Thackeray's Art and Morality," in *Critical Heritage,* p. 270.

8. John Carey, *Thackeray: Prodigal Genius* (London, 1977). See especially chs. 2–4.

9. Thackeray's use of things has been much discussed. See in particular Barbara Hardy's chapter, "The Expressive Things" in *The Exposure of Luxury,* pp. 95–117, and Juliet McMaster, "Thackeray's Things: Time's Local Habitation" in *The Victorian Experience,* ed. Richard Levine (Athens, Ohio 1976), pp. 49–86.

10. Walter Bagehot review of *Philip,* in *Critical Heritage,* p. 309.

11. The relevant passage in *Barry Lyndon* begins: "I believe a man forgets nothing. I've seen a flower, or heard some trivial word or two, which have awakened recollections that somehow had lain dormant for scores of years" (pt. 1, ch. 15).

12. Loofbourow, *Thackeray and the Form of Fiction,* pp. 205–14.

Selected Bibliography

PRIMARY SOURCES

1. Novels
   The entry cites the first book publication followed by the dates of the original serial run in parentheses.

The Adventures of Philip on His Way Through the World, Shewing Who Robbed Him, Who Helped Him, and Who Passed Him By. 3 vols. London: Smith, Elder, 1862. (*Cornhill,* Jan. 1861–Aug. 1862).

Catherine: A Story. London: Smith, Elder, 1869. (*Fraser's,* May 1839–Feb. 1840).

Denis Duval. London: Smith, Elder, 1867. (*Cornhill,* Mar.–June 1864).

The History of Henry Esmond, Esq. A Colonel in the Service of Her Majesty Queen Anne. 3 vols. London: Smith, Elder, 1852.

The History of Pendennis: His Fortunes and Misfortunes, His Friends and Greatest Enemy. 2 vols. London: Bradbury & Evans, 1849–50. (24 nos., Nov. 1848–Dec. 1850).

Lovel the Widower. New York: Harper, 1860. (*Cornhill,* Jan.–June 1860).

The Memoirs of Barry Lyndon, Esq. of the Kingdom of Ireland. London: Bradbury & Evans, 1856. (*Fraser's,* Jan.–Dec. 1844).

The Newcomes: Memoirs of a Most Respectable Family. 2 vols. London: Bradbury & Evans, 1854–55. (24 nos., Oct. 1853–Aug. 1855).

Vanity Fair: A Novel Without a Hero. London: Bradbury & Evans, 1848. (20 nos., Jan. 1847–July 1848).

The Virginians: A Tale of the Last Century. 2 vols. London: Bradbury & Evans, 1858–59. (24 nos., Nov. 1857–Oct. 1859).

2. Satires and Stories
   The following sections list some of Thackeray's most significant volumes aside from novels. For a more detailed list of his varied and extensive published writings, see Henry Van Duzer, *A Thackeray Library* (1919; reprint ed., Port Washington, N.Y.: Kennikat Press, 1965).

The Book of Snobs. London: Punch, 1848. (revised from *Punch,* Mar. 1846–Feb. 1847).

The Great Hoggarty Diamond. New York: Harper, 1848. (reprinted from *Fraser's,* Sept.–Dec. 1841).

Novels by Eminent Hands. London: Bradbury & Evans, 1856. (reprint of "Punch's Prize Novelists," *Punch,* Apr.–Oct. 1847).

The Second Funeral of Napoleon and the Chronicle of the Drum. London: H. Cunningham, 1841.

A Shabby Genteel Story. London: Bradbury & Evans, 1857. (reprint from *Fraser's,* June–Oct. 1840)

3. Essays and Lectures

The English Humourists of the Eighteenth Century. London: Smith, Elder, 1853.

The Four Georges. New York: Harper, 1860.

Roundabout Papers. London: Smith, Elder, 1863. (reprint from *Cornhill,* Jan. 1860–Nov. 1863).

The Paris Sketch Book. London: John Macrone, 1840.

4. Christmas Books

Dr. Birch and His Young Friends. London: Chapman & Hall, 1849.

The Kickleburys on the Rhine. London: Smith, Elder, 1850.

Mrs. Perkins's Ball. London: Chapman & Hall, 1847.

Our Street. London: Chapman & Hall, 1848.

Rebecca and Rowena: A Romance Upon Romance. London: Chapman & Hall, 1850.

The Rose and the Ring, Or, The History of Prince Giglio and Prince Belbo: A Fire-Side Pantomime for Great and Small Children. London: Smith, Elder, 1855.

5. Travel Books

The Irish Sketch Book. London: Chapman & Hall, 1843.

Notes of a Journey From Cornhill to Grand Cairo. London: Chapman & Hall, 1846.

6. Collected Journalism

Garnett, Robert S., ed. *The New Sketch Book. Essays Collected from the Foreign Quarterly Review.* London: Alston Rivers, 1906.

Ray, Gordon N., ed. *William Makepeace Thackeray: Contributions to the Morning Chronicle.* Urbana: University of Illinois Press, 1966.

Spencer, Walter Thomas, comp. *Mr. Thackeray's Writings for the "National Standard" and "Constitutional."* London: W.T. Spencer, 1899.

7. Collected Works

A standard edition of Thackeray's works is currently in preparation under the general editorship of Peter L. Shillingsburg at Mississippi State University. Meanwhile, the following are the most frequently cited editions:

The Works of William Makepeace Thackeray. Library Edition. 24 vols. London: Smith, Elder, 1867–69; 1886. First collected edition.

The Works of William Makepeace Thackeray. The Biographical Edition. 13 vols. New York and London: Harper, 1898–99. Enlarged as the Centenary Biographical Edition. 26 vols. 1910–11. Fullest edition to date and noteworthy for its biographical introductions by Thackeray's daughter, Anne Thackeray Ritchie.

The Oxford Thackeray. Edited by George Saintsbury. 17 vols. London: Oxford University Press, 1908. The most satisfactory in terms of text.

8. Correspondence

Ray, Gordon N., ed. *The Letters and Private Papers of William Makepeace Thackeray.* 4 vols. Cambridge, Mass.: Harvard University Press, 1945–46.

SECONDARY SOURCES

1. Bibliography

Flamm, Dudley. *Thackeray's Critics: An Annotated Bibliography of British and American Criticism, 1836–1901.* Chapel Hill: University of North Carolina Press, 1967.

Ford, George H., ed. *Victorian Fiction: A Second Guide to Research.* New York: Modern Language Association, 1978. Robert A. Colby surveys work done on Thackeray after Stevenson's review (below).

Olmstead, John Charles. *Thackeray and His Twentieth-Century Critics: An Annotated Bibliography of British and American Criticism, 1900–1975.* New York: Garland, 1977.

Stevenson, Lionel, ed. *Victorian Fiction: A Guide to Research.* Cambridge, Mass.: Harvard University Press, 1964. Contains a review essay by Lionel Stevenson on the state of Thackeray research.

2. Books and Parts of Books

The list of both books and articles is highly selective, concentrating on the more recent publications in the field.

Carey, John. *Thackeray: Prodigal Genius.* London: Faber & Faber, 1977. A lively study asserting that Thackeray's genius declined after *Vanity Fair* because of his surrender to his society.

Colby, Robert A. *Thackeray's Canvass of Humanity: An Author and His Public.* Columbus: Ohio State University Press, 1979. A thorough survey of Thackeray's entire canon, locating him firmly in the context of his time.

―――, ed. Special Thackeray issue of *Studies in the Novel* 13 (1981). Includes over a dozen original articles highlighting works and aspects of Thackeray often overlooked.

Ennis, Lambert. *Thackeray: The Sentimental Cynic.* Evanston: Northwestern University Press, 1950. Traces the workings of ambivalence in Thackeray's life and art. Organized biographically.

Garrett, Peter K. *The Victorian Multiplot Novel: Studies in Dialogical Form.* New Haven: Yale University Press, 1980. A theoretical study with a chapter examining how Thackeray replaces unitary meaning with a dialogue of perspectives.

Harden, Edgar F. *The Emergence of Thackeray's Serial Fiction.* Athens: University of Georgia Press, 1979. A detailed and patient analysis of how Thackeray worked with the demands of the monthly number.

Hardy, Barbara. *The Exposure of Luxury: Radical Themes in Thackeray.* Pittsburgh: University of Pittsburgh Press, 1972. A series of essays on the radical social criticism implicit in Thackeray's depiction of class and money.

Iser, Wolfgang. *The Implied Reader: Patterns of Communication in Prose Fiction From Bunyan to Beckett.* Baltimore: Johns Hopkins University Press, 1974. Includes a discussion of the active role of the reader in creating the meaning of *Vanity Fair* and a briefer analysis of subjectivity in *Henry Esmond.*

Knoepflmacher, U.C. *Laughter and Despair: Readings in Ten Novels of the Victorian Era.* Berkeley: University of California Press, 1971. Sees *Vanity Fair* as a "time-conscious and time-consuming" novel that both reflects and deliberately generates uncertainty.

Levine, George. *The Realistic Imagination: English Fiction from Frankenstein to Lady Chatterley.* Chicago: University of Chicago, 1981. A study of the complexities of Victorian realism, devoting three closely argued chapters to Thackeray's sophisticated awareness of the implications of realist assumptions.

Loofbourow, John. *Thackeray and the Form of Fiction.* Princeton: Princeton University Press, 1964. A landmark work, arguing for Thackeray as an innovator in developing a narrative medium to reflect the subjective nature of modern reality. *Henry Esmond* is the central text.

McMaster, Juliet. *Thackeray: The Major Novels.* Toronto: University of Toronto Press, 1971. Chapters on each major novel define Thackeray's main themes and techniques. Concludes with an important general essay on the psychological patterns of his fiction.

Miller, J. Hillis. *The Form of Victorian Fiction: Thackeray, Dickens, Trollope, George Eliot, Meredith, and Hardy.* Notre Dame, Ind.: University of Notre Dame Press, 1968. A suggestive exploration of novels as self-generating structures, focusing on the narrator in *Vanity Fair* and the hero in *Henry Esmond.*

Paris, Bernard J. *A Psychological Approach to Fiction: Studies in Thackeray, Stendhal, George Eliot, Dostoevsky and Conrad.* Bloomington: Indiana University Press, 1974. Analyzes relationships in *Vanity Fair* in light of Karen

Horney's psychological theories. Illuminates in particular the Amelia-Dobbin relationship.

Phillips, K. C. *The Language of Thackeray.* London: André Deutsch, 1978. Surveys such topics as Thackeray's use of slang, proper names, and modes of address, demonstrating his acute ear for the social and moral nuances of language.

Pollard, Arthur, ed. *Thackeray: Vanity Fair.* Macmillan Casebook Series. London: Macmillan, 1978. Useful collection that combines important twentieth-century comments with extracts from early reviews.

Rawlins, Jack P. *Thackeray's Novels: A Fiction That is True.* Berkeley: University of California Press, 1974. Stimulating interpretation of Thackeray's career as a search for alternatives to outmoded fictional conventions that ends in failure.

Ray, Gordon N. *Thackeray: The Uses of Adversity 1811–1846.* New York: McGraw-Hill, 1955. *Thackeray: The Age of Wisdom 1847–1863.* New York: McGraw-Hill, 1958. The definitive two-volume biography.

Shillingsburg, Peter L., ed. Special Thackeray volume of *Costerus,* n.s. 2 (1974). A gathering of articles and review essays emphasizing Thackeray's illustrations, textual scholarship, and bibliographic concerns.

Sundell, M. G., ed. *Twentieth-Century Interpretations of Vanity Fair.* Englewood Cliffs, N.J.: Prentice-Hall, 1969. A rather thin collection of standard essays.

Sutherland, J. A. *Thackeray at Work.* London: Athlone Press, 1974. Examines available manuscripts and concludes that Thackeray was a brilliant improvisator.

Tillotson, Geoffrey. *Thackeray the Novelist.* Cambridge: Cambridge University Press, 1954. Suggests that Thackeray's awareness of the "streamingness of experience" leads to his valuing continuity over design in his novels.

——— **and Donald Hawes, eds.** *Thackeray: The Critical Heritage.* London: Routledge & Kegan Paul, 1968. Valuable compendium of nineteenth-century reviews and essays.

Van Ghent, Dorothy. *The English Novel: Form and Function.* 1953; reprint ed., New York: Harper, 1961. Contains a classic essay on *Vanity Fair* as the depiction of a sick culture. Its celebration of Becky Sharp exemplifies an important tendency in the history of Thackeray criticism.

Welsh, Alexander, ed. *Thackeray: A Collection of Critical Essays.* Englewood Cliffs, N.J.: Prentice-Hall, 1968. A judicious selection of general and specialized articles, featuring a challenging introduction by Welsh.

Wheatley, James H. *Patterns in Thackeray's Fiction.* Cambridge, Mass.: M.I.T. Press, 1969. Suggestive but cryptic analysis of Thackeray's career as a shift in interest from the forms of literature to the forms used by individuals in life.

3. Articles

For articles dealing with more specialized topics and with Thackeray's lesser-known works consult Notes to the individual chapters. This list includes articles of more general interest and those representing significant critical trends.

Bledsoe, Robert. *"Pendennis* and the Power of Sentimentality: A Study of Motherly Love." *PMLA* 91 (1976): 871–83. Important insights into how Thackeray's exposure of the frustration of reality impels him to seek resolution on the level of fantasy.

Craig, G. Armour. "On the Style of *Vanity Fair."* In *Style in Prose Fiction.* English Institute Essays. Edited by Harold C. Martin. New York: Columbia University Press, 1959, pp. 87–113. Frequently reprinted, this essay explores the implications of Thackeray's inferential style.

DiBattista, Maria. "The Triumph of Clytemnestra: The Charades in *Vanity Fair."* *PMLA* 95 (1980): 827–37. Sophisticated feminist analysis of Thackeray's use of charades to image the dark and violent realities underlying civilized surfaces.

Garrett-Goodyear, Joan. "Stylized Emotions, Unrealized Selves: Expressive Characterization in Thackeray." *Victorian Studies* 22 (1979): 173–92. Focuses on *Henry Esmond* and *The Newcomes* to demonstrate how Thackeray's characterization conveys the pressure of intense impulses that elude expression and definition.

Hagan, John. *"Vanity Fair*: Becky Brought to Book Again." *Studies in the Novel* 7 (1975): 479–505. A rebuttal of arguments vindicating or excusing Becky, the essay provides a useful review of the controversy over Thackeray's heroine.

Harden, Edgar. "Esmond and the Search for Self." *Yearbook of English Studies* 3 (1973): 181–95. A thematic analysis of Esmond's search for identity, stressing the role of memory in self-definition.

Lester, John A. Jr. "Thackeray's Narrative Technique." *PMLA* 69 (1954): 392–409. Pioneering study of Thackeray's disruption of conventional linear narrative.

Lougy, Robert E. "Vision and Satire: The Warped Looking Glass in *Vanity Fair."* *PMLA* 90 (1975): 256–69. A compelling analysis of how *Vanity Fair* moves beyond satire to a "nightmare vision" of civilization itself as inherently diseased.

McMaster, Juliet. "Thackeray's Things: Time's Local Habitation." In *The Victorian Experience: The Novelists.* Edited by Richard Levine. Athens: University of Ohio Press, 1976, pp. 49–86. Gracefully surveys how things in Thackeray work to make concrete the passage of time.

McMaster, R. D. "The Pygmalion Motif in *The Newcomes."* *Nineteenth-Century Fiction* 29 (1974): 22–39. An important rereading of *Newcomes*, directing attention away from social themes to its concern with the problem of fiction-making.

Manning, Sylvia. "Incest and the Structure of *Henry Esmond.*" *Nineteenth-Century Fiction* 34 (1979): 194–213. Subtle psychological reading focusing on the father-son conflicts.

Mauskopf, Charles. "Thackeray's Concept of the Novel: A Study in Conflict." *Philological Quarterly* 50 (1971): 239–52. Thackeray's early comments on the novel reveal an incompatible view of fiction as at once mimetic and didactic.

Monod, Sylvère. " 'Brother Wearers of Motley,' " *Essays and Studies* 26 (1973): 66–82. Concentrates on *Pendennis,* analyzing the inconsistencies in narrative voice which make problematic the interpretation of Thackeray.

Ray, Gordon N. "*Vanity Fair*: One Version of the Novelist's Responsibility." In *Essays by Divers Hands: Being the Transactions of the Royal Society of Literature in the United Kingdom,*" n.s. 25 (1950): 87–101. Influential argument that Thackeray's reunion with his daughters in 1846 altered his concept of fiction and made possible the moral achievement of *Vanity Fair.*

Rogers, Katharine M. "The Pressure of Convention on Thackeray's Women." *Modern Language Review* 67 (1972):257–63. Argues that after *Vanity Fair,* Thackeray's attitude toward women became increasingly conventional.

Rogers, Winslow. "Thackeray's Self-Consciousness." In *The Worlds of Victorian Fiction.* Edited by Jerome H. Buckley. Cambridge, Mass.: Harvard University Press, 1975, pp. 149–63. Defines Thackeray's self-consciousness as an awareness that no perspective can be final.

Scarry, Elaine. "*Henry Esmond*: The Rookery at Castlewood." *Literary Monographs,* No 7. Edited by Eric Rothstein and Joseph A. Wittreich Jr. Madison: University of Wisconsin Press, 1975, pp. 1–45. Argues that the novel, after rejecting objective for subjective truth, undermines even the subjective truth it ostensibly affirms.

Segal, Elizabeth Towne. "Truth and Authenticity in Thackeray." *Journal of Narrative Technique* 2 (1972): 46–59. Draws attention to the paradox that realism motivates both Thackeray's authenticating devices and his exposure of the fictionality of his narrative.

Sheets, Robin Ann. "Art and Artistry in *Vanity Fair.*" *ELH* 42 (1975): 420–32. The novel dramatizes Thackeray's ambivalence about realist art, particularly in its handling of the unstable narrator.

Sudrann, Jean. " 'The Philosopher's Property': Thackeray and the Use of Time." *Victorian Studies* 10 (1967): 359–88. A rich meditation on Thackeray's temporal awareness and his use of memory to recover yet distance individual experience. Focuses on *Pendennis* and *Newcomes.*

Talon, Henri-A. "Time and Memory in Thackeray's *Henry Esmond.*" *Review of English Studies* 13 (1962): 147–56. Defines the significance of the retrospective stance in understanding and shaping the self.

Wilkinson, Ann Y. "The Tomeavsian Way of Knowing the World: Technique and Meaning in *Vanity Fair.*" *ELH* 32 (1965): 370–87. A key article on the novel, exploring the implications of its gossip-like technique for the notion of truth.

Index